THE DURA-EUROPOS SYNAGOGUE:
A RE-EVALUATION (1932-1972)

Edited by
Joseph Gutmann

Religion and the Arts 1

American Academy of Religion

Society of Biblical Literature

1973

THE DURA-EUROPOS SYNAGOGUE:

A RE-EVALUATION (1932-1972)

Edited by

Joseph Gutmann

Copyright © 1973

by

AMERICAN ACADEMY OF RELIGION
SOCIETY OF BIBLICAL LITERATURE

ISBN 0-88414-024-5

Library of Congress Catalog Card Number: 73-85879

Printed in the United States of America

Printing Department, University of Montana,
Missoula, Montana 59801

THE DURA SYNAGOGUE

Dura Synagogue: Southwest Corner, reconstruction in the
National Museum, Damascus

CONTENTS

LIST OF ILLUSTRATIONS[*]

* All Dura photographs are Courtesy of: Dura-
Europos Collection, Yale University. Our special
thanks to Dr. E. D. Francis, Curator of the Dura-
Europos Collection, for granting permission to
reproduce the photographs and for graciously
sending us new photos, figs. 1-5 and Frontispiece.

PREFACE

Discovered forty years ago in what Mikhail Rostovtzeff called "The Pompeii of the Syrian desert," the third-century Dura-Europos synagogue has successfully challenged stereotyped and well-established scholarly theories. Although not as well-known or as widely publicized as the Dead Sea Scrolls, the synagogue, nonetheless, has revolutionary implications of great importance to all students of ancient history, religion and art. The first major Jewish artistic monument ever to be unearthed, it contains the earliest known significant continuous cycle of biblical images. Figural decoration of similar complexity and extensiveness does not appear in Christian art until the fifth century.

To date the Dura synagogue has elicited more than ten major studies in English, French, German and Hebrew, by such outstanding scholars as Carl Kraeling, Erwin Goodenough and André Grabar, who concentrate primarily on the iconography - the meaning of individual scenes or of the entire cycle of paintings. As little monumental painting has been preserved from that period, art historians, such as Ann Perkins and Richard Brilliant, are trying to unravel the stylistic sources of these provincial works, in order to place them within the larger orbit of late

Roman art. At the same time Kurt Weitzmann and
Carl-Otto Nordström, among others, are continuing
their researches to determine the influence of the
Dura paintings or their models on later Christian art,
believing that behind the Dura paintings lie vast
cycles of lost Jewish illustrated manuscripts, without
which we cannot understand the surviving Old Testament cycles of later Christian art.

The Dura paintings have thus re-opened an older
debate in art historical circles - whether indeed the
origins of Christian art may be rooted in an antecedent, but now lost, Jewish art.

Since the amazing paintings of the Dura synagogue were hardly anticipated, or could be accounted
for, by classical Jewish or Christian historical scholarship, they have raised serious questions of the prevailing and accepted historiography of that period. In
particular, scholars must now undertake critical
re-evaluations of "normative rabbinic Judaism" and
the supposedly rigid iconoclasm of rabbinic Judaism,
which historians of Judaism presume flourished at
that time.

A major new discovery has not only widened
our horizons but posed tantalizing and difficult
questions outlined above. Our panel of scholars,
under the distinguished chairmanship of Clark
Hopkins, the field director of the Dura excavations,
have tried to examine these problems with fresh eyes

at the Los Angeles meeting of the International Congress of Learned Societies for the Study of Religion, held on September 4, 1972.

J. G.

INTRODUCTION

THE EXCAVATIONS OF THE
DURA SYNAGOGUE PAINTINGS

Clark Hopkins

Half way through the fifth season of excavations, conducted at Dura-Europos by Yale University and the French Academy of Inscriptions and Letters, in January 1932, we began clearing a building which lay close to the city wall. Several rooms of the structure had been freed from their cover in the embankment during the previous campaign, and the renewed digging quickly brought to light the Christian Chapel, an intrinsic part of the house partially excavated. It was this discovery that focused our attention on the rest of the great mound stretching along the whole course of the stone fortifications, thirty feet high, on the west side of the city.

A careful search of the slope north of the Main Gate revealed fragments of plaster adhering to mud-brick walls occasionally reaching the surface of the ground *in situ*, thus revealing the walls of buildings covered by the embankment. Of two rooms which seemed outlined by rectangular patterns in the position of these plaster fragments, the larger was chosen for excavation first in the Fall of 1932.

A shallow trench, six inches in depth, sunk along the facade of plaster, disclosed four walls of mud brick faced with plaster.[1] At the highest point in the northwest corner, there were splotches of color, irregular spots of dark brown, red, yellow and gray. M. le Comte du Mesnil du Buisson, assistant director of the excavations, took charge of this sector and began digging half way down the slope of the embankment toward the back wall in such a way that when the wall was reached, it would stand eight to ten feet above the base of the cut.

At this point we had no idea what one might expect when the rear wall of the room was reached. It seemed most probable that secondary walls would come to light dividing the building into rooms of more moderate size. On the plaster found around the whole perimeter of the room there was not a trace of painting other than the dots and dashes in the upper right hand corner. Nevertheless it seemed wise to take every precaution in view of the successive surprises that had already startled previous excavators at Dura.

Totally unexpected had been the discovery in 1920 of the great frescoes found by the British soldiers when a machine gun emplacement was dug in an angle of the circuit wall. A fortunate chance had brought an expedition of the Oriental Institute of the University of Chicago to Mesopotamia at that time, and Professor J. H. Breasted and his staff were able to establish, as the result of a long day's work (before the retreat of the soldiers began), that the paintings dated from the first century of our era, and that they embraced fundamental concepts of Byzantine art: the tall figures, the strict frontality, the staring eyes and the stylized folds of the robe.[2]

A painting of a Roman cohort sacrificing to the three great male gods of the desert pushed the Roman frontier forty miles south of Circesium, formerly considered the southern Roman frontier on the Euphrates, and so forty miles south of the confluence of the Khabour and the Euphrates. The sky gods, represented above the *Tyches* of Palmyra and Dura, suggested the title of "The Temple of Palmyrene Gods."[3]

When Dura was placed in the French mandated territory of Syria by the treaty of San Remo in 1920, the opportunity to excavate at Dura was first offered to the University of Chicago, then taken up by the French Academy under the leadership of Franz Cumont. The French Foreign Legion began explorations and Monsieur Cumont, with the aid of the legionaires, in the course of two short fall seasons, uncovered more frescoes in the Temple of Palmyrene Gods and explored the Temple of Artemis in the center of the city. In a tower close to the British excavations some parchments were recovered, pre-

serving records of the original Greco-Macedonian
clereuchs who founded the city about 300 B.C., as a
half way station between the Seleucid capitals at
Antioch on the Orontes and Seleucia on the Tigris.[4]
More important, the parchments proved that at least
in certain areas of the city, normally perishable
materials were preserved almost as well as in Egypt.

After the Druse rebellion of 1925-6, permission
to continue the excavations was granted to a
French-American expedition, under the directorship
of Prof. M. I. Rostovtzeff, and financed by Yale
University through the generosity of the General
Education Board. With Monsieur Maurice Pillet as
Field Director, the first four seasons, 1928-31, sup-
plemented the finds made by the English soldiers
with the Oriental Institute, and by the French Legionaires. Very notable progress was made with valu-
able finds: important buildings, significant inscriptions. In the fifth campaign came the astounding discovery of a Christian Chapel, built in the first half of
the third century,[5] containing the earliest Christian
paintings in the Eastern Mediterranean. This discovery furnished the final proof that the embankment preserved both walls and paintings.

In the Fall and early Winter of 1932, the season
after discovery of the Christian Chapel, as we came
closer and closer to the rear wall of the new building,
it became evident that the whole space belonged to

one big room. The paintings at Dura are not frescoes
with the colors embedded in the plaster but made in
tempera and so easily blurred if incautiously rubbed.
To protect the side walls, therefore, a foot of dirt was
left standing in front, as long as the digging toward
the rear continued. When the limits of the room had
been reached, dirt completely covering the paintings
remained until the cut might be evenly completed
and the whole wall might be disclosed at once. A
combination of good weather and the early part of a
work week of ten days was required for the best opportunity to remove the dirt cover.

Still there was no indication, no inkling of the
revelation to come. The day of action was fixed
upon. There were the enthusiasts and the sceptics, the
optimists and the pessimists. There was the wall forty
feet long and the cut extending ten to twelve feet
beneath the surface, a bare blank wall of dirt, packed
down, but easily undercut to fall away without im-
pairing the plaster surface. Overhead the same bright
sun that had greeted us so many mornings in the past,
shone through the early morning coolness, 45-55
degrees; very little wind, a perfect late Fall day.

The signal was given and the best of our pick-
men undercut the blanket of dirt concealing the west
wall. Like a blanket or a series of blankets the dirt fell
and revealed pictures, paintings, vivid in color, startling; so fresh it seemed they might have been painted

a month before. There was a mighty series of paintings, the scenes continuing from the north corner
along the whole forty feet of wall.[6]

The work in other trenches almost stopped!
Members of the expedition, not already there, were
hastily summoned. It was a scene like a dream! In the
infinite space of clear blue sky and bare gray desert,
there was a miracle taking place, an oasis of painting
springing up from the dull earth. The size of the room
was dwarfed by the limitless horizons but no one
could deny the extraordinary array of figures, the
brilliant scenes, the astounding colors. What did it
mean? Who was this tall figure leading a host from
the fortress walls of a city, and what meant those
splotches of red and yellow above the walls in the
high corner of the painting?[7]

In Aramaic between the feet of the great leader
was written, "Moses leads out of Egypt."[8] If the
paintings were spectacular enough by themselves the
Aramaic inscription fixing the scene was a
heaven-sent gift. Who would believe that in this desert
fortress, this frontier town, this third century caravan
city, there should have been and still was preserved a
Synagogue, its great walls covered with paintings?
What had seemed like the random daubs of paint in
the upper corner, became the plagues of fire and hail
descending on the walls of Egypt and the heavenly
guides for the host, the pillars of smoke and fire were

carefully included though on the wrong side of the Israelite forces.

In that first year we hesitated to dig down farther, lest the wall with its precious paintings collapse. We could not resist, however, digging a narrow trench to the center of the rear wall and we uncovered the central niche, the Torah shrine with the sacred symbols and the scene of Abraham and Isaac.[9] Before the season was over, large painted ceiling tiles of baked brick provided the names of Jewish leaders and the date A.D. 244-45.

Even in an expedition such as Dura, however, life is not all the delight of discovery! With the spectacular find comes the responsibility. We were fortunate indeed, in having Monsieur du Mesnil, a Captain in the French reserve, as a liaison with the French Command in Deir-ez-Zor, and in finding in the French army the understanding and generosity of Colonel Gounouneix and his staff, who provided the materials for a roof of corrugated metal to protect the paintings. Experience with the paintings of the Temple of Palmyrene Gods had given us acquaintance with the transparent varnish which fixes the powdery colors to the walls. Application of the varnish restores momentarily a brilliance to the paintings. The original colors had dulled during the days spent in carefully removing bits of dust and earth adhering to the surface. Once again when the transparent varnish was applied, the colors blossomed magnificently, then faded again, or rather lost their fresh lively aspect. It was very much like the effect of water on a stone mosaic floor; then the return of the more sombre colors as the water evaporates.

Our architect, Mr. Henry Pearson, was able to cut away the mud brick backing of the wall, to reinforce the back of the gypsum plaster with lime mortar, strengthened with fibre and with wooden struts. The upper wall was gradually removed and each piece as it was taken out was photographed from exactly the same position and distance, so a photographic mosaic of the whole wall was reconstructed years before the reconstruction in Damascus provided the first view of the Synagogue in its entirety.

The division of finds was not easy at a time when an equal apportionment of all moveable discoveries was to be effected between the Syrian Government and Yale University. There was naturally the determination to keep all the paintings together; and to restore if possible, the whole building to include the roof tiles of the ceiling and the columns of the court. On the one side there was the Christian Chapel, with its paintings, small but most interesting; on the other side the paintings of the Synagogue, tremendous in size and still more interesting.

Fortunately the discovery of the temple of Mithra in the following season allowed a division acceptable to both: with Yale taking the Christian Chapel and the Mithraeum, Syria the Synagogue. Still more fortunately the construction of a new museum in Damascus gave opportunity to reconstruct both the Synagogue room and its court; to build the rest of the museum around this magnificent display,[10] and restore in drawing the original sanctuary (Frontispiece).[11]

There are two footnotes essential to this account. The continued clearing of the embankment not only disclosed the temple of Mithra, the painted wooden shields of the Roman defenders and the papyri records of the Camp, but also details of the final unsuccessful defense of the city.

The embankment had been constructed in a last desperate effort to repel the Persian attack in A.D. 256. It failed in its purpose, but providentially for us it encased and preserved at least in part the Synagogue, the Christian Chapel, the Mithraeum, three other temples and an amazing display of wooden objects, parchments, papyri, cloth and metal.

When the Bollingen Foundation assisted Professor E. R. Goodenough in publishing the *Jewish Symbols in the Greco-Roman Period*, the photographs of the Synagogue paintings were not considered quite adequate for the illustrations. Mr. Fred Anderegg was sent, therefore, from the University of Michigan to secure a new set of photographs in Damascus. He found the lighting difficult but dis-

1. C. H. Kraeling, *The Excavations at Dura-Europos, Final Report VIII, 1, The Synagogue* (New Haven, 1956), pl. I, 1.

2. J. H. Breasted, *Oriental Forerunners of Byzantine Painting I* (Chicago, 1924), pl. IX.

3. F. Cumont, *Fouilles de Doura-Europos* (Paris, 1926), pl. L.

4. M. I. Rostovtzeff, *Dura-Europos and its Art* (Oxford, 1938), 2, fig. 1.

5. C. H. Kraeling, *The Excavations at Dura-Europos, Final Report VIII, 2, The Christian Building* (New Haven, 1967), pl. XXIV.

6. *L'Illustration* (July 29, 1933), 457.

7. *The Excavations at Dura-Europos, Preliminary Report of the Sixth Season of Work* (New Haven, 1936), pl. LII.

8. Comte R. du Mesnil du Buisson, *Les peintures de la Synagogue de Doura-Europos* (Rome, 1939), pl. XVIII.

9. *L'Illustration, op. cit.,* 457.

10. Rostovtzeff, *op. cit.,* pl. XXI.

11. *Ibid.,* pl. XX.

12. E. R. Goodenough, *Jewish Symbols in the Greco-Roman Period XI* (New York, 1964), pl. I (Bollingen Series XXXVII, Vols. 9-11, *Symbolism in the Dura Synagogue*).

PAINTING AT DURA-EUROPOS
AND ROMAN ART*

Richard Brilliant

Dura Europos has preserved the largest body of ancient wall-paintings from the classical period outside of Italy. Since their preliminary, tendentious publication by J. Breasted fifty years ago, despite the subsequent discoveries of the Yale University-Académie des Inscriptions et Belles-Lettres excavations in the 1920's and 1930's, the paintings themselves have never been studied as a group of works, potentially coherent and created over two centuries by artists of modest talent, exposed to diverse pictorial traditions. The predominantly religious subject matter and programs of these paintings, reflecting the faith of their patrons and the importance of images in the places of worship, have diverted attention away from these monuments as works of art, as paintings subject to critical, visual analysis and characterization. Partial attempts have been made to do so by Franz Cumont, Marcel Aubert, le Comte Robert du Mesnil du Buisson, Rachel Wischnitzer, Erwin Goodenough, André Grabar, and Carl Kraeling, but most of their efforts have been directed toward the establishment of connections between the Dura paintings and early medieval art or were preoccupied with iconographic questions at the expense of formal analysis. Yet the history of these paintings as paintings requires equal attention to their composition, employment of motifs, uses of color and line, principles and patterns of design, and stylistic evolution. Only through a critical description of their visual appearance is it possible to characterize these paintings properly, identify their properties, and attempt a stylistic definition of painting at Dura. Unfortunately, determining what they are is contaminated by considerations of what they are like, a conceptual problem that arises from Dura's cultural and artistic relationships with its environment. Here, the provincial character of Dura and the nature of Greco-Roman art in the eastern Mediterranean become central issues.

Thirty-seven years ago M. Rostovtzeff published his monographic article on "Dura and the Problem of Parthian Art" in *Yale Classical Studies* (1935) and conceptualized many of the critical problems in the analysis of Dura, the diverse inhabitants of the city, and their art. He and others who have studied Dura drew attention to the complex cultural mix in the city population, to the varying intensities of cultural and artistic influence, and to the contradictory, hybridizing environment of this community on two frontiers. For Rostovtzeff, the art of Dura was a northwèst variant of Parthian art in Mesopotamia,

specifically affected by the presence of
non-Mesopotamian ethnic groups, and especially by
the Palmyrenes. Despite the historical validity of his
thesis, the difficult, diffuse nature of Parthian art
itself remained ill-defined, while the related arts of
Palmyra, of the Nabataeans, and of Roman Syria
were beginning to be better known as the result of
archaeological exploration. Furthermore, the phe-
nomenon of provincial art as a problem of criticism
and terminology was unappreciated, witness the un-
certainties in treating the regional or localized artistic
productions of hellenized western and central Asia or
the controversy over the Greek or Roman sources of
the analogous art of Gandhara.

Since World War II, the French scholars Henri
Seyrig, Roman Ghirshman, and Daniel Schlumberger
have worked extensively in this area and have con-
tributed to our comprehension of the diversity of
Parthian art and other local styles, nicely charac-
terized by Schlumberger in his term, "l'orient
hellénisé," which emphasizes their non-Mediterranean
foundation. Advances in this field were also signalled
by the title of a conference held in 1965 at the
Accademia dei Lincei in Rome, "La Persia e il mondo
Greco-Romano," while the hieratic conventions of
hellenized oriental art were treated as cognate, even
participatory factors in the development of western
art at another Lincei conference (1967), entitled

"Tardo antico e alto medioevo." Much of this movement toward a more secure conception of the history
of art in Mesopotamia and Syria during the Roman
period was stimulated by the work of Gerhart
Rodenwaldt and the Italian scholars, Silvio Ferri,
Doro Levi, Antonio Frova, Guido Mansuelli, and
Ranuccio Bianchi Bandinelli who began to deal with
normative problems in Roman Imperial art. In particular, they sought to characterize Roman provincial
art in its diverse regional manifestations as well as in
its metropolitan phases. It is within this enriched
critical situation that the paintings of Dura must be
presented.

Such an analysis mandates the establishment of
precise distinctions among the constituent elements
of the paintings, leading in turn to the identification
and characterization of the degrees of relationship
between them in Dura and their counterparts elsewhere within a temporal, cultural horizon. In order to
do this as thoroughly and as objectively as possible, I
am developing an abstract, extended method of
analysis, presented diagrammatically in the form of
an inventoried flow-chart. The chart serves to isolate,
identify, categorize, and connect these elements in an
effort to define diagnostically the intrinsic character
of art at Dura, if any, and also to specify the orienta-
tions of its provinciality or dependence. Briefly, the
kinds of elements that have been selected for analysis

consist in part of the following:

I. Motif
  a. *the half-reclining figure,* as seen in "Elijah receiving the Widow's Child" (Dura Synagogue) . . . counterparts in Palmyra, Etruscan sarcophagus lids, Roman painting, "Sleeping Ariadne" type, other Dura examples.
  b. *the frontal, seated king, with legs crossed, knees pointing outward,* as used for David, Ahasuerus, Pharoah in the Dura Synagogue and in Iranian art.
  c. *seriatim groupings* (of different types), as in "Samuel anoints David" (Dura Synagogue) . . . counterparts in paintings from Temple of Palmyrene Gods (Dura), Palmyrene reliefs, Gandhara, Sacrifice panel in Arch of Septimius Severus (Leptis Magna).

II. Compositional Patterns
  a. *iconistic frontality,* in numerous examples in painting and sculpture (Dura) . . . counterparts in Palmyra, Hatra, Parthia, Roman tomb reliefs from Italy and the Rhineland, Column of Marcus Aurelius, Triumphal Panel in Arch of Septimius Severus (Leptis Magna).
  b. *specificity and frontality,* as in the Sacrifice of Konon from the Temple of the Palmyrene Gods (Dura) . . . counterparts in Palmyrene tomb paintings, Fayum portraits, Pompeian portraits, Roman, I/II century A.D., altar reliefs.
  c. *graffitto and outline,* in numerous examples at Dura . . . counterparts in many Roman provincial monuments from Danube to Britain, Catacomb paintings, Late Antique metal work.

III. Themes
  a. *epiphany,* as in the Ezekiel panel (Dura Synagogue) . . . counterparts in Early Christian art, Appearance

of Miraculous Rain in Column of Marcus Aurelius,
Roman, II-IV century, coin reverses (e.g. *providentia)*
b. *majesty*, abundant examples.

IV. Programs
   a. *the terminal wall: epiphany and predellas*, as in the
   west wall of the Dura Synagogue . . . counterparts,
   Temple of Zeus Theos (Dura), Hypogeum of the
   Three Brothers (Palmyra), Mithraea at Dura and elsewhere, Roman triumphal arches (figs. 1-5).

There are many other items, such as costume,
pose, scale, parataxis, isocephaly, halo, panel orientation and sequence, scenic division, landscape and
hunting conventions, space, color patterns and
palette, etc. Each of these is to be used as a topic of
investigation into painting at Dura, and specifically as
well to demonstrate the connections between Dura
and the artistic communities and sources to which it
relates. In this way the adaptive process which seems
to characterize the art of Dura can be made explicit,
while the analysis will clarify the degree of independence as a discrete local style to which Duran art
evolved from adaptation through hybridization. One
should not forget, however, that the paintings at Dura
were executed by local artists of very modest ability
working in pictorial idioms familiar in the area and
exhibiting varying amounts of dialectal localization,
dependent ultimately on the hybridized traditions of
the hellenized orient on the western edge of Parthia.

Thus, the Greco-Roman features these paintings reveal are for the most part either chance intrusions or indirectly derivative through the pre-existing hybrid style of the region. At a preliminary level of analysis, it appears that the paintings at Dura do not constitute an example of Roman provincial art, despite the fact that most of them were executed while the city was under Roman rule, because the lines of stylistic and elemental dependency do not exist with sufficient directness, frequency, or consistency. A strong connection does exist between some of the paintings, especially from the Synagogue, and Roman Imperial art at a deeper level of formal generation, suggested by their mutual dependence on hieratic compositions and teleological narratives. If this relationship, however, is only sympathetic, then no stylistic and historical bond exists between them. The question still remains, whether Dura ever attained the status of a distinct provincial style in relation to Parthian art, if there is such a thing in some pure state, or whether because the region itself was fundamentally a hybridized culture on a semitic-iranian base no such resolution was possible. If that is so, then Parthian art possesses no core but rather reveals itself in a very broad spectrum of adaptation, of which Dura forms a representative but not very distinct part. A very close analysis of the paintings as a whole should give the answer, and in context.

HYPOTHETICAL MODELS OF THE DURA PAINTINGS

Mary Lee Thompson

In 1941 Karl Lehmann prefaced his analysis of the *Imagines* of the Elder Philostratus with a slighting reference to the Synagogue at Dura. Philostratus' descriptions of the paintings should be analyzed as real, existing works, he said, especially as they belong to the third century, which may be called the dark age of ancient paintings - a period when preserved works are so scarce that middle class tombs are used as the cornerstone of the history of painting, and "the discovery of the frescoes of a Jewish synagogue in Mesopotamia tends to revolutionize the entire picture."[1] Lehmann went on to show that Philostratus saw the paintings arranged in five rooms in a villa near Naples, forming programs of cosmic, philosophical and theological nature, with possibly Neo-Pythagorean inspiration for the entire complex.[2]

The insight into religious programs through ancient literary description is the other side of the coin minted by Erwin Goodenough in analyzing mystical symbolism in a room full of very real, equally startling paintings found at Dura. It is fitting that Goodenough dedicated a section of his study of

Jewish symbols to Karl Lehmann.[3]

The task of this paper is not to interpret the meaningful programs that exist in domestic or cult rooms, but to inquire what is the mode of transmission of motifs, pictures and combinations of pictures across time and place in the Roman Empire. In my work on the programs found in houses in Pompeii I assumed that painters used repertory or pattern books from which pictures could be copied and programs devised.[4] In a survey of all rooms in Pompeii with two or more paintings, it is evident that there is a similarity in the manner of composing programs and the types of programs. The individual paintings are variable: the same picture can be copied and used in different combinations. One does not find absolutely identical programs; hence I assumed that pattern books existed for single pictures, and it was simply common practice to use certain kinds of programs. For instance, of the 277 rooms analyzed in my dissertation, the programs of 185, or two-thirds, center on Dionysus and Aphrodite and their domains. Therefore, presumably, the house owner and his decorator decided in each case which pictures would be used in programs focusing on these gods, or on the deeds of heroes, or moralizing illustrations of divine reward and punishment. The execution of the paintings varies greatly in quality, and also they reflect different stylistic prototypes.[5]

This brings us to the question of how the vastly more elaborate and profound program at the Dura Synagogue was composed. What was the relation of the decorator to his patron and to the painters who executed the various parts? Did they have model books to draw upon for details, for whole scenes, or even for the manner of combination of scenes into a program? In Kraeling's publication of the Synagogue he refers to the artists, or those who commissioned the work, as choosing the subjects and their juxtaposition; he also mentions the difference in identifiable hands and suggests a master working with assistants.[6]

While Kraeling prefers to speak of the "artists" and not to speculate on the procedure of creation or execution, Goodenough's interpretation of more elaborate symbolism leads him to assume that there was a director of iconography, who was not necessarily a painter. The direction could even, he suggests, have been by a committee of such men as those named in the ceiling tiles.[7] He uses the title "Philosopher" for the chief planner, citing an ancient account of a stonecutter's workshop in which those in charge are called thus. He takes philosopher to mean designer and suggests that his role was probably the symbolic development and expression. He further attributes the poor execution of the Dura paintings to the executing painters who were not up to the ele-

vated concepts of the Philosopher. He glimpses the
working procedure of the painters in the many
changes in the reredos, as they repeatedly tried to
satisfy the ideas of the Philosopher. He stresses the
role of the Philosopher as an originator, as the inven-
tor of the Dura program, rejecting the usual suggestion that the paintings are derived from earlier
sources. He emphasizes this point saying:

> Indeed, I suspect that the history of art has been
> altogether too much concerned with finding
> archetypes, after the mistaken analogy of fam-
> ilies of manuscript tradition from an ultimate
> original autograph of an author. That there were
> standard reproductions of a few hellenistic
> original statues must not obscure the fact that,
> generally in antiquity, individual artists, or the
> designers directing them, worked with a voca-
> bulary of symbols somewhat, again, after the
> analogy of medieval workers. Ancient artists, I
> am sure, made their designs by combining recog-
> nized symbols. Each artist, or directing bishop,
> or "philosopher," instructed the craftsmen in
> the design, or if he was a miniaturist, himself
> predesigned it, and in the design, in spite of his
> established vocabulary of symbols, he expressed
> his own creative impulses.[8]

Goodenough thus disclaimed the importance of
archetypes and the method of much art historical
research, particularly referring to the type of work

done by Kurt Weitzmann in the study of manuscripts. Nonetheless, Goodenough himself, and most others, point out elements of style and iconography whose archetypes must have been transmitted by some unspecified means. For instance, Goodenough identified the reclining Elijah as Dionysus and traces the history of the motif in earlier art. He identified the Pharaoh's daughter as Aphrodite-Anahita as represented in other art of the East and even in Dura itself.[9] It seems logical that the designer and painters had some mechanical aid, such as sketches or cartoons to transcribe the motifs. Kraeling, in his more practical approach, sees less originality and more use of archetypes. He actually does speak of the need to assume that pattern books allowed the Dura artists to use such traditional iconographic and stylistic elements as stage space, cartographic combined with frontal representation, cast shadows of a certain sort, stereotypes of figure poses, and groups such as the audience scenes, Greek type dress, armour and representations of pagan statues, temples and city walls.[10]

Beyond the enumeration of these details, Kraeling considers the possibility that there were painted synagogues in upper Mesopotamia or eastern Syria that might have provided the model for the provincial copy at Dura.[11] If there were, then of course one need not assume pattern books that pre-

served a repertory of motifs, but rather artists who
were sent specifically to the hypothetical source to
prepare the copy, with the aid of sketches or cartoons. Since there is no actual evidence for these pre-
ceding synagogues that might have served the Dura
painters as a specific model, Kraeling does not press
the point, and opts for manuscripts as the font of
pictorial material. For the actual practice of painting
a cult room with tiers of aretological scenes, focused
on a central shrine of the deity, Kraeling sees
self-explanatory precedence in the many pagan
shrines and the Christian chapel in Dura itself.[12]
While part of a local tradition that was presumably
well known in Dura, as was the basic scheme of
composing known in the town of Pompeii, another
proposal has been made by Georg Kretschmar that
the wall unit of side scenes flanking a central one was
a scheme repeated via pattern books in Dura (the
Torah shrine and the flanking figures of Moses) as
well as in the decorations of distant sanctuaries such
as San Vitale in Ravenna and the church of the
monastery of St. Catherine on Mount Sinai[13] (fig. 1).

It is important to note that these suggestions
presume that the source for the Dura cycle is, ultimately, other monumental pictorial works, be they
mosaics or wall paintings. While painted temples are a
special feature of Dura, most of our knowledge of
ancient painting and mosaics is from houses. The

possibility that Old Testament iconography was derived from decorations in Jewish homes has not found favor,[14] however Kraeling does propose that the dado frieze of animals and theatrical masks derives from secular decoration, that the basic framework of the decorative divisions of the wall is related remotely, to earlier domestic (and funereal) tradition.[15] I would not exclude the possible existence of religious decoration in houses as arbitrarily as Kraeling does. He says, "The Christians and the Jews both of Dura and of Rome were altogether too clear in their understanding of where it was and was not appropriate to represent biblical scenes to make it likely that they were ever widely used for the sheer embellishment of private dwellings."[16] While Kraeling does cite the underground basilica at Porta Maggiore, the Villa of the Mysteries at Pompeii, and the many Mithraea as examples of programmatic painting of religious character antecedent to the examples at Dura,[17] I would add that these cult rooms are domestic whether in style or location. Additional noteworthy examples are the Hall of Aphrodite from Boscoreale and the room devoted to Dionysus in the House of Marcus Lucretius [IX, 3, 5 (16)] in Pompeii, as well as the complex of rooms seen by Philostratus.[18] Likewise, though some of these examples actually were cult rooms, the majority of domestic programs in ordinary living rooms was

also didactic and moralistic in a religious way. It is
well to remember the role of the family and its home
as the basis of Roman religion. Hence I emphasize the
points in common between the Dura Synagogue
paintings and earlier domestic decoration. While I do
not go as far as Karl Schefold in attributing mystical
character to the domestic programs (just as I prefer
Kraeling's matter of fact approach to Goodenough's),
domestic decoration should not be rejected as an
antecedent. It seldom was "sheer embellishment."[19]
Doro Levi's study of the mosaics from Antioch shows
many examples of philosophical and religious concepts used in houses even closer to the Dura paintings
chronologically and geographically.[20] In fact, I find
an antecedent to the didactic character that Kraeling
sees in Dura in Roman domestic decoration, even in
the stress on divine reward and punishment.[21]

Next, let us consider the hypothesis of illuminated manuscripts as the source of the pictorial cycles
at Dura. Since the Synagogue was painted in a period
when the papyrus scroll was the major book form,[22]
the usefulness of manuscripts to the artists of the wall
paintings was limited. The nature of the task of illustrations on papyrus rolls is not comparable to the
task of the wall painter in composing large panels, nor
much less whole programs. While Goodenough allows
a relation to manuscript tradition only in details such
as the representation of the Ark, Kraeling favors the

hypothesis of biblical illustrations as the main source, stressing the close relation of the scenes to the literary narration, episode by episode.[23] He uses Weitzmann's system of analyzing omission, condensation and conflation as evidence of use of the more numerous images presumed in a manuscript source. Kraeling almost wins me over with the ingenious suggestion that the right to left general movement of the story in the painting of the "Infancy of Moses" is combined with a left to right movement of the individual figures - the former being due to the location of the scene on the wall, and the latter to the derivation from a Greek, rather than an Aramaic manuscript (fig. 5). Despite this observation, I am not persuaded by the hypothesis that manuscript illustrations were the literal source of the Dura paintings. Kraeling does, however, make a strong point of the importance of the very existence of a divine book as an impetus to the narrative programs of Jews and Christians. This, he says, may help to explain the character of the art shared by both, with symbolic and narrative purpose coexisting from the very start.[24] This existence of a single divine book also explains the difference from Pompeii where Roman domestic programs do not echo the arrangement of a literary narrative, and do not derive from illustrated manuscripts. In fact they actually avoid logical narrative sequence. For instance though many episodes

suasively that the most famous of these Roman friezes, the Odyssey landscapes, is actually an accurate copy of an earlier Hellenistic wall painting.[29]

Just as I am skeptical of the idea that manuscript illumination was the "pattern book" for Roman wall painting, so I do not believe it to be the explanation of the program of the scenes at Dura, or of its variety of style and composition. It was once suggested by Karl Lehmann that this variety was introduced to Dura via the use of a manuscript which contained illustrations with different styles of space representation. (This opinion was only quoted from a lecture of Lehmann and so far as I know he did not pursue it).[30] Both Weitzmann's studies on the nature of ancient book illustrations, and Bianchi Bandinelli's proposal that this kind of combination of sources exists in the Ambrosian Iliad, show that this could not have occured as early as the first half of the 3rd century A.D. in Dura.[31]

If manuscript illustrations prior to the period of the Dura paintings were primarily line drawings of small format on papyrus scrolls, such illustrations should not be assumed to be the source of a monumental cycle such as that in the Synagogue. Scholars of a generation before mine have always stressed the poor quality of the wall paintings. My own impression is that they are effective monumental compositions, belonging to the realm of major art.

Hence I find most congenial the idea that their ante-
cedents must be found in monumental art, and similarly, that in the third century wall painting is still the
major art and hence the current of influence goes
from it to the lesser art of manuscripts, not the reverse.[32]

If one does not accept book illustration as the
source for Roman wall painting in Pompeii, or Dura,
and yet one finds repetition of motifs, compositions
and even indication that the original was of higher
quality than the copy, then how did ancient artists
make copies and preserve traditional ways to
compose, symbolize and narrate? As far back as
1939, Du Mesnil du Buisson suggested that there were
models. He cited several examples in early Christian
mosaics and manuscripts where similarities to the
Dura compositions suggest lost prototypes, which
have continued to preoccupy Weitzmann in his
studies of pictorial transmission. Indeed, Weitzmann
promised a detailed study of the relation of Dura to
manuscripts. Du Mesnil did not see the prototypes as
necessarily biblical however. He felt that the compositional elements could have just as well come from
pagan paintings via *carnets de croquis.* He pointed
out, too, the repetition of figures which suggest the
use of cut-out models, that is cartoons.[33] We have
already described the more recent suggestions that
some kind of models were used at Dura. Models, car-

toons or pattern books have also been suggested to explain the wide diffusion of identical or similar compositions in mosaics.[34] As an example of copies which suggest the use of pattern books in painters' or mosaicists' workshops I would like to refer to a group of paintings of "Aphrodite Fishing" from Pompeii which by their very monotony (20 examples) and mediocrity have suffered physical as well as scholarly neglect.[35] The compositions and their combination in programs vary, but poses and details are found again and again. The fact that the paintings are not of high quality enforces the impression of copy-book repetition. The theme is limited to Campanian painting, but it is representative of the manner of repetition and the availability of a composition for recombination in various contexts.

While cartoons and pattern books have been suggested often in modern scholarship there is a dearth of ancient literary sources that might shed light on the workshop procedures. There is one ancient reference to the fact that copies were indeed made: a copy of a picture of Pausias, called an apographon, is cited by Pliny.[36] Modern authors have not gone on to speculate how copies ·were actually made, or what pattern books and cartoons might have looked like. There were drawings on papyrus that served as patterns as we know from two examples found in Egypt and published by Scheller as the preface to his book

on medieval model books. One of these is of the first
century B.C. and is a sheet of drawings of figures of
humans and animals and architectural details; the
other is of the 4th to 6th century A.D. and gives the
design for a coptic textile. Scheller points out the sad
fact that the absence of a real drawing book preserved
from ancient times should come as no surprise as the
remnants of classical libraries are so few. Indeed, it is
even less likely that there would be remnants of the
contents of a decorator's shop. Scheller also makes a
suggestion that may be valid for ancient procedures as
well as medieval, that there could also have been
preparatory drawings done on wax tablets, which
would be erased as soon as the need had been
served.[37]

Line drawings of the small scale permitted by the
nature of papyrus would aid in the composition of
figures and groups, but could not preserve the full
pictorial or painterly character of paintings. Is it
possible that panel paintings preserving the nuance of
color, light and shade were part of the artists' reference collection to be consulted whether making wall
paintings or mosaics, or even manuscripts? We know
from representations of panel paintings on Pompeian
walls that this was a medium for copying. Encaustic
painting on wooden panels was transportable and
could even travel to the job, or from site to site. We
have already spoken of Hellenistic cycles of panel pic-

tures known from literary sources. Phyllis Lehmann suggests that such were the prototype of the Hall of Aphrodite from Boscoreale, and this is also the unique case of the wall paintings including an imitation of a panel painting that must have been the actual source for the wall painting as a whole.[38]

The kind of workshop aid implied by cartoons means something different from the small sketch possible on papyrus or the detailed and rich image preserved on an encaustic panel painting. If cartoons were used actually to aid in transferring images, as they are in post-Renaissance fresco painting, we must imagine a medium that permits a much larger scale. I would like to propose that our knowledge of ancient triumphal painting provides the clue. These paintings must have been done on cloth stretched on a wood framework so they would be light enough to be easily moved, and large enough to permit the extensive scenes that are described in ancient literature on triumphal art.[39] Cloth with painting or drawing on it seems the most likely form of the cartoons used for copying pictures or mosaics. It would be practical as being relatively inexpensive and expendable.

To bring the argument full circle, it seems that not only must we acknowledge the existence of pattern books and cartoons as methodologically necessary and materially possible within the ancient technology of painting and mosaic, but that it is also quite possible that such pattern books served the painters who for the first time were illustrating vellum codices. The versatility of such pattern books was suggested in a review of de Wit's study of the Vatican Virgil: Hugo Buchthal felt that the painters could have used "a model book where the figures and the buildings already belonged together - a composition that did not represent anything or anybody in particular, and could be used whenever it was wanted and for whatever subject it fitted" - Dido reproaching Aeneas or whatever. Even Weitzmann suggests that panel paintings played a roll in the enrichment of codex illustrations to include the landscape backgrounds current in earlier art.[40] A doctoral dissertation by Thomas Stevenson, recently done under Buchthal, carries the study of the sources of the miniatures in the Vatican Virgil much further. He finds, again and again, evidence of borrowings from the common repertory of representations in fourth century art in all media, and believes that pattern books served as the means of transmission.[41]

In conclusion, pattern books, panel paintings and cartoons must have been standard equipment of ancient artists. They were in use at least from Hellenistic times onward, and while ephemeral they must have been ubiquitous. Pattern collections drawn on papyrus had a resemblance to illustrations in book rolls but they must have been a distinct genre.

Manuscripts were expensive and not likely to be knocked around in a painter's studio, or on the job. Pattern books could have been used by the potters who made the Homeric bowls, and the sculptors who made the Iliac tablets, as Harry Bober pointed out. Similarly, pattern books, panels and cartoons, copied and copied again, served wall painters in Dura as they had in Pompeii, and were probably around even during the 9th and 10th centuries A.D. when, as Kurt Weitzmann has shown, the artists of the Macedonian Renaissance were echoing Hellenistic and Roman art.[42]

*My gratitude to Pamela Steele and Karyl Gottlieb, two students at Manhattanville College, for help with bibliography.

1. K. Lehmann, "The *Imagines* of the Elder Philostratus," *Art Bulletin* 23 (1941), 16-44, esp. 17.

2. *Ibid.*, 43.

3. E. R. Goodenough, *Jewish Symbols in the Greco-Roman Period* V-VI (New York, 1953-1956).

4. M. L. Thompson, "The Monumental and Literary Evidence for Programmatic Painting in Antiquity," *Marsyas* 9 (1960-1961), esp. 46.

5. M. L. Thompson, "Programmatic Painting in Pompeii, the Meaningful Combination of Mythological Pictures in Room Decoration," Unpublished Ph.D. thesis (University Microfilms 60-5299), New York University, 1960, 221, 63ff. Thompson, *Marsyas* 4 6.

6. C. H. Kraeling, *The Synagogue* (New Haven, 1956), 356f. 380.

7. Goodenough, *op. cit.*, IX, 22.

8. *Ibid.*, 186.

9. *Ibid.*, XII, 167f. with ref. to previous vols.

10. Kraeling, *op. cit.*, 368-370, 379-380, 382f.

11. *Ibid.*, 392.

12. *Ibid.*, 348f.; Kraeling, *The Christian Building* (New Haven, 1967), 218f.

13. G. Kretschmar, "Ein Beitrag zur Frage nach dem Verhältnis zwischen jüdischer und christlicher Kunst in der Antike," *Abraham unser Vater, Festschrift für Otto Michel* (Leiden, 1963), 295-319. Reprinted in J. Gutmann, ed., *No Graven Images, Studies in Art and the Hebrew Bible* (New York, 1971), 156-184. K. Weitzmann, "The Mosaic in St. Catherine's Monastery on Mount Sinai," *Proceedings of the American Philosophical Society* 110 (1966), 392-405.

14. R. Comte du Mesnil du Buisson, *Les peintures de la Synagogue de Doura-Europos* (Rome, 1939), 143. Kraeling, *The Christian Building*, 216.

15. Kraeling, *The Synagogue*, 240ff., 250.

16. Kraeling, *The Christian Building*, 216.

17. *Ibid.*, 157.

18. P. W. Lehmann, *Roman Wall Paintings from Boscoreale in the Metropolitan Museum of Art* (Cambridge, Mass., 1953). Thompson, *Marsyas* 66, figs. 5A-I.

19. K. Schefold, *Pompejanische Malerei, Sinn und Ideengeschichte* (Basel, 1952). K. Schefold, *Vergessenes Pompeji, unveröffentlichte Bilder römischer Wanddekorationen in Geschichtlicher Folge herausgegeben* (Berne and Munich, 1962).

20. D. Levi, *Antioch Mosaic Pavements* (Princeton, 1947).

21. Kraeling, *The Synagogue*, 349, 357.

22. K. Weitzmann, "Book Illustration of the Fourth Century: Tradition and Innovation," *Studies in Classical and Byzantine Manuscript Illumination*, H. L. Kessler, ed. (Chicago, 1971), esp. 102f., 96-125.

23. Goodenough, *op. cit.*, X, 12. Kraeling, *The Synagogue*, 365, 388ff., 394f., 398. K. Weitzmann, "The Illustrations of the Septuagint," *Studies*, 45-75, esp. 71, 75. K. Weitzmann, "Narration in Early Christendom," *American Journal of Archaeology* 61 (1957), 83-91, esp. 89.

24. Kraeling, *The Christian Building*, 221.

25. Thompson, *Marsyas* 40, n. 16; Thesis, 67ff.

26. K. Weitzmann, *Illustrations in Roll and Codex; a Study of the Origin and Method of Text Illustration* (Princeton, 1970), 23, 27ff. Weitzmann, *Ancient Book Illumination* (Cambridge, Mass., 1959), 64, 69ff. Kraeling, *The Synagogue*, 399ff.

27. Thompson, *Marsyas* 51f.

28. Weitzmann, *Ancient Book Illumination*, 37ff.; *Roll and Codex*, often. Schefold, *Pomp. Mal.*, 82; *Vergessenes Pomp.*, index "Bilderbuch"; K. Schefold, "Origins of Roman Landscape Painting," *Art Bulletin* 42 (1960), 87-96. R. Bianchi-Bandinelli, *Hellenistic-Byzantine*

Miniatures of the Iliad, Ilias Ambrosiana (Olten, 1955), 31.

29. P. H. von Blanckenhagen, "The Odyssey Frieze," *Mitteilungen des Deutschen Archäologischen Instituts, Römische Abteilung* 70 (1963), 100-146.

30. E. Hill, "Roman Elements in the Setup of the Synagogue Frescoes at Dura," *Marsyas* 1 (1941), 1-15, esp. 3, n. 13.

31. Weitzmann, *Roll and Codex;* Bianchi-Bandinelli, *op. cit.,* 28.

32. J. Gutmann, "The Illustrated Jewish Manuscript in Antiquity, the Present State of the Question," *No Graven Images,* 232-248, esp. 233f. Bianchi-Bandinelli, *op. cit.,* 28, 30.

33. Du Mesnil, *op. cit.,* 149; Weitzmann, *op. cit.,* 1970 ed. addenda, 228.

34. Levi, *op. cit.,* 8f., with bibliog., 624; Bianchi-Bandinelli, *op. cit.,* 11.

35. Thompson, Thesis, 158-167; Schefold, *Vergessene Pompeji,* 80, 174.

36. Pliny, *Natural History,* XXXV, 125. For a discussion of panel paintings and their display see A. W. Van Buren, "Pinacothecae," *Memoirs of the American Academy in Rome* 15 (1938), 70-81; Van Buren, "Pinacotheca," *Paulys Realencyclopädie,* Supplementband VIII (1956), 500-502.

37. R. W. Scheller, *A Survey of Medieval Model Books* (Haarlem, 1963), 2, Cat. No. 1 and 2.

38. Lehmann, *op. cit.*, 144f.

39. K. Lehmann-Hartleben, *Die trajanssaule, ein römisches Kunstwerk zu Beginn der Spätantike* (Berlin and Leipzig, 1926), index Triumphmalerei; Ch. M. Dawson, *Romano-Campanian Mythological Landscape Painting* (New Haven, 1944), 50-52 with bibliog.

40. H. Buchthal, "Review of J. de Wit, *Die Miniaturen des Vergilius Vaticanus,*" *Art Bulletin* 45 (1963), 373-375. Weitzmann, *Roll and Codex*, 100.

41. T. B. Stevenson, "The Miniatures of the Vatican Virgil," Unpublished Ph.D. thesis, New York University, 1970, esp. 121-137.

42. H. Bober, "Review of K. Weitzmann, *Roll and Codex,*" *Art Bulletin* 30 (1948), 284-288. Weitzmann, "The Character and the Intellectual Origins of the Macedonian Renaissance," *Studies*, 176-223; Weitzmann, *Roll and Codex*, addenda to 1970 ed., 228.

THE DURA SYNAGOGUE COSTUMES
AND PARTHIAN ART

Bernard Goldman

Considering the richness of the material remains of the Dura synagogue, which offer an almost endless variety of historical, religious, and artistic questions, most of which are still unanswered, a word of explanation is in order for devoting time to a modest detail, the tailored suits worn by some of the actors in the mural narratives. As a mode of costuming, as a clothing fashion, it is distinct from draped wear that also appears in antiquity: the himation, toga, kilt, robe, etc. The tailored suit—a sleeved tunic or jacket worn over trousers—is not rare, although it is a relatively recent form of dress in the Orient that has been documented in its several appearances. By the third century A.D., when both styles of dress appear together in the synagogue murals, the tailored and the draped costumes had come to represent two worlds, that of the Orient and that of the Mediterranean respectively. The tailored suit became fashionable in the last centuries of the Old Orient, for the earlier and more pervasive form of dress had been draped robes, kimono-like garb, skirts, and kilts. The source of the trousered costume has often been laid at the

doorstep of northern Eurasia, for it appears to have
been particularly suited to the activities of horse-
riding people in the cold, sub-arctic climate.[1] By the
turn of the millennium it was clearly *the* Parthian
costume.

That both trousered suits and draped robes
should appear in the synagogue murals is not in itself
surprising, but, none-the-less, has demanded explanation: why do some figures affect the Oriental style of
dress while others prefer the Mediterranean and is
there a meaning far beyond the casual in that selec-
tion? The answers given by both Goodenough and
Kraeling made choice of costume one of the keys to
the over-arching problems of the synagogue murals
that continue to worry commentators: the identification of figures and scenes, and, thus, the interpretation of the sequences or cycles of paintings; the posit-
ing of an *Ur*-source for the pictorial narratives. Hence,
a brief review of the fashion of tailored suits in the
Orient is helpful, although, admittedly, it will not in
itself solve the dilemmas posed.

Goodenough suggested that the anonymous
artists of the synagogue, or their program director,
cloaked those figures of a holy nature in the draped
robe *(himation, pallium)* of white ("white" as the
symbolic equivalent of "light" with its mystic over-
tones of the divine).[2] The trousered costume he suggested as being used without any symbolic signifi-

cance, usually worn by people of modest importance except when a cape or coat *(chlamys, kandys)* was added as a mark of the regal court and the king himself (fig. 6). Kraeling marked the tailored suit as the "court costume," the habitual dress of kings and their entourage as well as the garb of temple personnel.[3] Rostovtzeff in his first broad discussion of the art of Dura Europos noted that five basic types of dress were worn in the synagogue murals but he did not discuss them within an iconographical context.[4]

Thus, on the basis of choice of costume—tailored or draped—both Goodenough and Kraeling were able to suggest identities for some of the figures not otherwise readily identifiable, and could thereby substantiate the location of the biblo-historical event in which they were depicted. This all too brief summary of the views and reasoning of the two magisterial scholars implies a far more rigid appearance than 'either intended; Goodenough clearly stated the dangers of rigidly adhering to a separation of holy and princely, of spiritual and mundane leaders, on the basis of dress alone. He also warned against any system of arguing which would show " . . . by studying the paintings that the Greek costume means this, the Persian that, then to explain the paintings on that basis, and finally to complete the circle by showing that the paintings have in turn explained the dress . . . "[5] But he also used the type of costuming as a significant element in establishing the iconography.

There are no contemporary writings to confirm the ascription of costumes; although some fabrics have been uncovered, in themselves they do not establish symbolic meanings of different modes of wear but rather the financial status of the wearer and the sex.[6] On the basis of internal evidence alone—that is, the synagogue paintings themselves—it is obvious that some of the robed figures are holy men and sacred, while, equally, some of the men wearing trousered suits are of the royal court. But no more general observation than that can be drawn from an inspection of the murals, for there is also to be found figures who are in secondary roles wearing the robes just as there are trousered suits on figures who are not connected with the court or royalty. (Being concerned only with any light the trousered suit may shed on the iconography and sources of the murals, I omit from discussion the dress of the women, the military costumes, and the short tunics or *chitons* worn by children, servants, and laborers). Kraeling and Goodenough suggested and exploited one type of approach to the use of costume, an approach that eventuated in some fairly specific conclusions about the identity of the actors and the scenes in which they appeared and about the kind of source material that may have been behind the synagogue murals.

Another approach to costumes, based upon the contemporary and near contemporary use of the tailored
suit in the Orient, suggests a different set of circumstances and, hence, different conclusions. I set out, in
somewhat skeletal form, this structure below.

The draped robes portrayed in the synagogue
murals, along with other pictorial conventions therein
contained, are directly based upon the styles patented
by Western, Classical tailors and introduced into the
Orient with the physical intrusion of Hellenism—
military, political, and social, in that order historical-
ly. But draped robes did not first come into the Near
East with Alexander's troops in the fourth century
B.C.; several styles of draped gowns, as distinguished
from the fitted and sleeved wraps or kimono-like
dress of Assyria and Babylonia, were popular prior
to the domination of Alexander and the Hellenistic rulers. Typical examples are those worn by
the Hittites and royal Achaemenians, but their robes
are of a distinctly different cut than that of the Greek
himation or Roman *pallium*. It is true that certain
similarities in the handling of drapery by Achaemenian sculptors on the one hand, and Greek artists
on the other in the later decades of the sixth century
B.C. have raised questions as to whether Persian
robing may not have been indebted to Greek dress-
making ideas (via Ionian, Carian, Lydian contacts?).[7]

Fortunately that sorely contested problem and its possible resolution are not crucial to the fashions found several centuries later at Dura. What is pertinent, however, is that immediately prior to Hellenistic rule in the East, the dominant political house of the Orient, the Achaemenian, habitually wore two types of dress, the draped robe and the trousered suit. The Persian side of the royal entourage affected the robe while the wearing of tunic and trousers marked the Medians of the confederation. But if both types of costume appeared in the Achaemenian halls of Persepolis, the royal family always and only wore robes, at least as far as we may determine from the sculptured images, over life-size in rock reliefs to miniatures on coins and seals. Xenophon spoke of Persian trousers, but he indicates a robe worn over them: " . . . Cyrus himself made his appearance . . . having on his legs loose trousers of a scarlet color, and a robe wholly purple." (*Cyropaedia* VIII, iii, 13). The sky-borne god who floats on high in Achaemenian art wears the same draped costume as his royal, mundane representative. In the carvings at Bisitun, Naqsh-i Rustam, and Persepolis variations in the two basic types of dress identify not the position or character of the wearer, but rather his geographical place of origin.[8]

Thus costume fashions of the Achaemenian world are not distinguishable according to sacred and adopt, on occasion, the dress of his newly acquired Oriental domain, a practice that earned him the rebuke of his counselors.[11] His reasons for so doing may have sprung from a dream of one-world, or from the practical politician's goal of augmenting his charismatic image in the eyes and minds of his constituents by outwardly identifying with them (as does the modern campaigner, adopting hard hat, top hat, and ten gallon hat in his regional excursions). However, the descriptions of Alexander's foreign affectations do not include the trousered suit and jacket: "Then he put on the Persian diadem and dressed himself in the white robe and the Persian sash and everything else except the trousers and the long-sleeved upper garment " (*Diodorus of Sicily* XVII, lxxvii, 5). We can only guess at the reason for this exception, but it is highly likely that it sprang from the fact that trousers were the mark of the foreigner in the Orient and hence they would interfere with integrative designs. Alexander, we are assured by Plutarch, " . . . did not adopt the famous Median fashion of dress, which was altogether barbaric and strange, nor did he assume trousers or sleeved vest . . . " (*Lives: Alexander* XLV). And Alexander must have been equally sensitive to the fact that in the eyes of the Asiatic, recently freed from the domination of the Achaemenian royal household, the robe still represented semi-divine authority, the mark of the king.

Thus there is good reason to view the long tradition of robes in the Orient as providing this form of dress with a significance beyond the ethno-political descriptive: rulers, both cosmic and temporal, and the draped robe were united.

To what extent did the post-Alexander inheritors of the old Persian sphere accept and continue this tradition? The Parthians were the first to challenge successfully on a large scale the Hellenistic rulers of the East and to re-establish, albeit on a severely reduced scale, Achaemenian political hegemony. The next and more enduring power to rise was the Sasanian monarchy which, unlike its Parthian predecessors, claimed direct connections with the long since overthrown Achaemenian royal household, thereby establishing a degree of legitimacy for its territorial and political ambitions. The Parthians replaced Hellenistic rule in the regions they dominated, but they did not despise the manners of their Hellenistic foes. The remains discovered at the first Parthian capital of Nysa (or Nisa, in modern Soviet Turkmenistan) are thoroughly Hellenized, even as the Parthian rulers adopted Greek titles and epithets.[12] Clark Hopkins, who uncovered the Dura synagogue, also found the remains of the slow transition in Parthian art and architecture from Hellenistic domination to Parthian innovation in his excavations of the Parthian level at Seleucia-on-the-Tigris. The

Parthians, of course, popularized the tailored costume in the Orient: it has come to be referred to as the Parthian costume.

The Sasanians, while aligning themselves with the old Achaemenian power complex, did not accept the Persian kingly robe, despite its regal associations. Rather, they continued in use the tailored wear introduced into Iran by the Parthians. Flowing robes were reserved for Sasanian women. Why the Sasanians chose the tailored dress as royal garb, counter to Oriental tradition wherein the robe ruled *par excellence*, is peripheral to the question at hand, but not without interest. That the reason is not based on a sacred-secular, holy-regal distinction seems clear, for as the Sasanian kings adopted trousers, so also did their gods, as evidence, for example, in the Sasanian reliefs of Naqsh-i Rustam, Firouz-abad, and Taq-i Bustan.[13] I suggest two primary reasons for the preference for the tailored suit: 1) the general historical pattern in Western Asia shows a steady movement away from Graeco-Roman influence over the centuries as Hellenism began its Eastern decline, and 2) as the wearing of the Mediterranean robe indicated obeisance to Western culture, so the Parthian suit became in itself a gesture of independence from the Graeco-Roman colonialism against which the Sasanians successfully fought.

The tailored costume of the synagogue walls

consists of somewhat loose trousers tucked into soft boots (fig. 7). The upper part of the body wears a tunic that reaches, usually, to the knees, is long-sleeved with a round neck-line, and has side vents from hem to waist which is girdled with a belt. A long-sleeved coat is worn sometimes over the tunic, perhaps as a mark of status for it is affected by figures that otherwise can be identified as major personnages: the enthroned Ahasuerus and Pharoah, Mordecai in triumph, and David. Only the priest Aaron (next to him is written his name in Greek characters) wears a great cloak in the synagogue murals, made of heavy material encrusted with what may be precious stones and pearls, far different from the light, fluttering shoulder capes worn elsewhere over tailored suits (fig. 8). A large brooch or clasp fastens the priest's cloak at his chest. Although unique at Dura, the cloak was probably a product of a Parthian tailor for it also appears in the Sasanian relief at Taq-i Bustan.[14] Some of the actors in the murals wear more loosely fitting trousers than do others, the pant legs blousing over the tops of the boots. But the differences of tight and loose trouser legs are due to the circumstances of drawing rather than to changes in style. For example, the seated Ahasuerus is shown with one pant leg tightly drawn, the other full and blousing. Tucked into the tops of soft boots, the Durene trousers never achieve the structure operating in the murals.

I find at least three strong deterrents to the whole-hearted acceptance of any theory of iconography of dress at Dura that involve not only the interpretation of costume but also the reading of the murals in general and, indeed, the reading of all ancient Judaic art. They may best be stated in the form of questions, for they are queries and not dicta.

These questions are not immediately answerable, although it is reasonable to doubt, without contrary evidence, that the artists hired by the Dura Jews were steeped in iconographical lore and symbolism, or that the small community was burdened with such understanding. And, as Joseph Gutmann points out, manuscript illustrations that could be used as the prototypes for the murals do not now, at least, exist in fact, but have been hypothesized to satisfy the need for an *Ur*-source.[14a]

I suggest, therefore, that the choice of costumes in the murals has been freighted with too inflexible an iconographical role, and that the dress may not be a trustworthy guide to identification of person or story. Rather, a less restrictive view of choice of clothing may be in order, one that takes into account the provincial nature of the border community and the types of sources that the artists turned to for models, for it appears that they cast their net more broadly, encompassing more than a single *Ur*-source.

1. Given that Durene Jewry formed a small enclave in this commercial caravan town of the hinterlands, far removed from the centers of Jewish population and learning, can we assume *a priori* that the artists hired by the elders of such a community to decorate their synagogue would be schooled in the profound pictorial symbolic intricacies that have been ascribed to the murals?

2. Or, if we assume the existence of Jewish artists working in the provinces who have the necessary insight and learning, or the presence of a hypothetical erudite religious director of the paintings who would work out so delicately constructed an iconographical scheme, can we also assume that the Dura Jewish community was sufficiently sophisticated to seek out workmen who could develop for them elaborate iconographical conceits?

3. Or, lastly, if we assume that the iconographical and symbolic complexities ascribed to the murals were simply part of a general, standardized, easily exportable pictorial format, copied over and over again by artists who had long since forgotten the meaning of the symbols they portrayed, for communities equally innocent of the hidden meanings their paintings held, do we have any tangible evidence to support the existence of the hypothecated models or originals—illuminated manuscripts? Jewish copybooks? Haggadic illustrations?

The most extensive accumulation of narrative art, in the form of deep-cut reliefs, comes from Gandhara, which displays a sharp distinction in the use of robe and tailored costume (the native Indian dress, the dhoti, sanghati, etc., is of course the most common, but not to the point here). The Bodhisattva wears neither, for he clothed himself in native garb of befitting princely splendor, as did the supramundane figures, courtly retinues, etc. But he placed this aside when he attained Enlightenment, and put on the simple draped robe. The Buddha never, to my knowledge, appears in a tailored, trousered costume, nor do his followers. It has been suggested that part of the reason behind the Buddha's choice of costume in Gandharan art lies in the association of the teacher with the Classical robe. Perhaps this symbolism may provide one of the reasons why the single, standing figures flanking the Torah Shrine at Dura, regardless of their identity (Moses? Ezra? Abraham?), whose frontal positions and attitudes mark them as preceptors, wear the robes. The tailored suit appears in Gandhara—trousers, tunic, soft boots or slippers, and sometimes a sleeved coat—where it is reserved for the outsider. Thus are dressed the Kushan donors worshipfully standing in sacred scenes, but also similarly clothed are Iranians and Asiatics who may fill no more important role than that of musician, dancer, or guard. Essentially, at Gandhara, as in Greece, the these divine figures also appear clad in robes. There is, of course, an obvious difficulty encountered when comparing use of costume at different places: the possible differences imposed by the social status of the various figures. I am particularly conscious of this factor at Hatra, for there the sculptural representations are of upper class groups while in the synagogue paintings there is represented a wide range of classes.

In Asia Minor, at Nimrud Dagh of the first century B.C., we find, as may be expected, a pronounced combination of West and East because, first, of the early date of the sculpture, and, second, because of the geographical location that insured close ties with the Mediterranean sphere. Thus, the trousered costume is a relative rarity. A different type of affluent dress is current in the district, however, a long robe drawn up by a cord between the legs so as to offer some of the freedom of movement normally permitted by trousers. Similarly, Nabataea graphically illustrates in its sculpture its sturdy Western veneer, adopting the draped robe to the exclusion of the tailored suit.[16]

Parthian illustrations from the Iranian highlands are meager in number. The noble, over life-size bronze from Shami, probably of the second century B.C. (now in the Tehran Musée Bastan), has been clad in trousers and jacket, and the protective over-pants that resemble somewhat the Western American chaps,

called *jambières* (leggings or leg guards) in the literature.[17] While the wind-blown cloak found in the
synagogue murals also appears on figurines of
Parthian riders, the *jambières* never are worn by the
Dura figures. And at Dura the pullover tunic is pre-
ferred to the jacket. Afghan sculpture, such as that
from Hadda and Surkh Kotal, wears the same type
dress as that of Dura, including the sleeved coat.[18]
The jacket worn by the Shami bronze is not merely
the precursor of the tunic, and replaced by it; the
jacket must have been the standard fancy dress style
in the eastern reaches of the Parthian realm, lingering
on into Sasanian and post-Sasanian times of Central
Asia as distinctly courtly dress.[19] The Parthian cele-
brant, probably priestly, making an incense offering
on the free-standing rock at Bisitun wears the tailored
costume girdled with a heavy belt of a type found at
Hatra but not used by the Durenes. Later, in the
second and third centuries A.D., Parthians wear
heavily draped trousers, beginning the fashion that
will be exploited by Sasanian stylists, as on the relief
from Susa of Artabanus V (215 A.D.), and the noble
on the little Parthian relief in Berlin.

This very brief review confirms some basic
principles in regard to the appearance of the tailored
suit. The farther removed a locality is from inter-
course with the Hellenic West, the more fashionable is
the trouser costume; whereas, the corollary holds,

that the more cosmopolitan a community, the greater
the association with the draped robe. As the political
fortunes of Hellenism waned in the East and the
Oriental substratum vigorously reasserted itself, costume fashions swung to the Oriental. Both styles of
dress lived comfortably side by side, not only at
Palmyra, Seleucia-on-the-Tigris, and Dura, but also in
Parthian Iran itself, as the Hellenized bronze statuary
from the shrine at Shami indicates. Such conclusions
strongly suggest that as different modes of dress
become habitual and common-place in one community they lose much of whatever symbolic depth
they may have had. To say that costume was largely a
reflex of the socio-political scene does not entail the
complete abandonment of its iconographical importance. But it does indicate that to establish a strict
symbolic role for choice of costume in the synagogue
murals is to permit one aspect to cloud over and
almost completely obscure the historical realities of
dress fashions in the Near East.

Hence, I suggest that the artists of Dura may not
have followed any hypothetical programming of costume symbolism or have absorbed unwittingly, perhaps, a consistent iconography of fashion by rote
copying of suspected but as yet unknown Jewish
illuminated manuscripts. The synagogue artists were
skilful, admittedly, more adept at organizing and pro-
jecting complex visual narratives than, say, the

painter of the Dura chapel, but lacking in the pictorial imagination of Pompeiian artists or even (if
comparisons ought to be drawn only from the Orient)
of the Iranian artists at Kuh-i Khwaja or of the somewhat later painters of Central Asia. The synagogue
artists display vigor and clarity in delineation of the
individual figures; their instinct for narration is keen,
an inheritance of the most ancient pictorial tradition
of the Orient. But their organization of compositional
units is strained and awkward, unarticulated in a
manner that strongly suggests the painters utilized
stock types and formats which, in turn, were the
sources of the type of costume used in any particular
element.

1. Single standing, large-scale figures were clothed
in robes, a format taken directly from Classical sculpture, as found also in Gandharan art. The robe carried
with it the aura of teacher and philosopher; it stood
for dignity and spiritual solemnity when worn by the
single, statuesque figure. Such sculptural models were
everywhere to be seen, for the Oriental artist to know
and memorize and copy; he needed no single specific
prototype.

2. Some figures arrayed in stock poses could and
did wear either costume. For example, Elijah as
healer wears the robe when he reclines upon his
couch, a standard pose found in Greek art on Western
Asiatic soil centuries before Dura, as early as the

Lydian funerary monuments depicting the deceased on their *kline*.[20] The format had been adopted at Palmyra where the costume of the reclining figure was optional, a good example of a Hellenic pictorial device lodged in the Oriental visual "vocabulary." So also at Dura the standard pose is used for figures in tailored suits, such as in the so-called Saul and David in the wilderness scene. How stereotyped is this pose in the East in Parthian and post-Parthian times is indicated by, for example, its use in the Tang-i Sarwak relief of *ca.* 200 A.D. and on the Sasanian silver plate.

3. Court scenes are stock pictorial compositions: enthronement indicated secular power in the Orient, and Oriental kings from late Parthian times and on wore trousers; so also, then, do rulers on the synagogue walls, be they Jewish (David), Egyptian, or Persian, or, as in the Dura Mithraeum, a Magus. The type continues in an almost identical format in Sasanian art well along in the sixth and seventh centuries A.D.

4. While scenes of strong activity are not common at Dura, except for those of battle where military dress is portrayed, groups of actively engaged figures are drawn in tailored costumes. On the other hand, when stacked rows of figures are depicted in the over-lapping ranks that hark back to Roman format (*viz.* scenes of Exodus, prophets of Ba'al, Samuel

annointing), robes are the standard garb. The reason for this latter convention is not difficult to find: simple adoption of the ubiquitous Roman compositional type.

5. A general air of solemnity and gravity attaches itself to the draped robe, to a large extent because of its long tradition of use, compared to that of the tailored suit. Hence, unless other pertinent considerations interfere (such as: Oriental potentates wear trousered costumes despite their majesty, in late Parthian times), the robe is employed for the sense of dignity with which it is viewed.

This suggested pattern for choice of costuming in the synagogue implies that the artists did not work from complete picture models—prototype illustrations—but rather that they selected individual figures and groups of figures that were stock units in the arts of the time. These visual clichés, or idiomatic expressions were probably learned by heart by apprentice painters and composed into pictures at the artist's choice. And perhaps it is due to this mode of composition, which is a very common way of creating pictures, that we know of nothing exactly comparable to the synagogue paintings in the Parthian sphere, but yet find the individual units out of which the scenes are constructed to be so very familiar.

1. See G. Widengren, "Some Remarks on Riding Costume and Articles of Dress among Iranian Peoples in Antiquity," *Studia Ethnographica Upsaliensia* 11 (1956), 228-276; A. Foucher, *L'Art gréco-bouddhique du Gandāra*, II (Paris, 1918), 94.

2. E. R. Goodenough, *Jewish Symbols in the Greco-Roman Period* IX (New York, 1964), 124-126; E. R. Goodenough, "The Greek Garments on Jewish Heroes in the Dura Synagogue," in A. Altman, ed., *Biblical Motifs, Origins and Transformations* (Cambridge, 1966), 221-237.

3. C. H. Kraeling, *The Synagogue, Excavations at Dura-Europos, Final Report* VIII, 1 (New Haven, 1956), 71-72; contra, Goodenough, *Jewish Symbols, op. cit.*, 129, note 41.

4. M. I. Rostovtzeff, *Dura-Europos and Its Art* (Oxford, 1938), 117.

5. Goodenough, *op. cit.*, 124.

6. Cf. Y. Yadin, *Bar-Kokhba* (New York, 1971), 67-72, 76.

7. B. Goldman, "Origin of the Persian Robe," *Iranica Antiqua* 4 (1964), 133-152; G. Thompson, "Iranian Dress in the Achaemenian Period," *Iran* 3 (1965), 121-126.

8. On the various opinions held on regional costumes in Achaemenian art, see now, G. Walser, *Die Völkerschaften*

auf den Reliefs von Persepolis (Berlin, 1966).

9. There are, as with all rules, possible exceptions. Cf. the enigmatic stone figurines in the Foroughi Collection (Tehran) and the Louvre, A. Parrot, "Statuette méso-potamienne archaïque," in K. Bittel, *et al.*, *Vorderasiatische Archäologie* (Berlin, 1964), 230-233: do they wear chain mail leggings, or trousers, or fish scales, or mountain symbols?

10. The best Greek illustration of the Persian court, in Median dress however, is that on the so-called "Vase of the Persians" of the fourth century B.C. now in the National Museum, Naples. H. Schoppa, *Die Darstellung der Perser in der griechischen Kunst bis zum Beginn des Hellenismus* (Heidelberg, 1933).

11. E. Neuffer, *Das Kostüm Alexanders des Grossen* (Giessen, 1929), 10ff.

12. D. Schlumberger, *L'Orient hellénisé* (Paris, 1970), 34ff.; M.-L. Chaumont, "Les Ostraca de Nisa," *Journal asiatique* 256 (1968), 11-36.

13. See the fine study by E. H. Peck, "The Representation of Costumes in the Reliefs of Taq-i-Bustan," *Artibus Asiae* 31 (1969), 101ff.

14. A. Godard, *L'Art de l'Iran* (Paris, 1962), pl. 113.

14.[a] J. Gutmann, "The Illustrated Jewish Manuscript in Antiquity," in *No Graven Images* (New York, 1971), 232-48.

15. D. Homes-Fredericq, *Hatra et ses sculptures parthe* (Istanbul, 1963), 21-26.

16. Convenient summary in C. Vogelpohl, "Die griechische-römischen Wurzeln," Münchner Stadtmuseum, *Die Nabatäer* (Munich, 1970), 11-15.

17. H. Seyrig, "Armes et costumes iraniens de Palmyre," *Syria* 18 (1939), 10-14.

18. B. Dagens, M. Le Berre, and D. Schlumberger, *Monuments préislamiques d'Afghanistan* (Paris, 1964), pl. x, No. 4.

19. A. Grünwedel, *Alt-Kutscha* (Berlin, 1920), figs. 11-12; D. Schlumberger, "Descendants non-Mediterranéens de l'art grec," *Syria* 37 (1960), 62ff.

20. R. Thönges-Stringaris, "Das griechische Totenmahl," *Mitteilungen des Deutschen Archäologischen Instituts, Athenische Abteilung* 80 (1965), 1-99.

THE ARCHITECTURE OF THE DURA
AND SARDIS SYNAGOGUES

Andrew Seager

The Dura synagogue is important not only for its wall paintings but for its architecture as well. The paintings have received much of the attention, but the building too is provocative and in many ways unique. The excavation reports[1] present architectural evidence concerning such important issues as 1) the origins of ancient synagogue architecture and its evolution during the later Roman Empire, 2) the orientation of worship in synagogues, 3) the provision for women at worship, and 4) the functions of the courtyard and annex rooms.

Much of the interpretation of that evidence is based on comparisons between the Dura building and the group of synagogues in Galilee traditionally dated to the late second and early third centuries A.D. The Dura building differs significantly from the synagogues of the "Galilean type" both in general appearance and in some important details.[2] Neither does the Dura structure closely conform to the model of the "later" or "Byzantine type" of synagogue which succeeds the Galilean type, according to the usual interpretation, beginning about the fourth century A.D.[3]

More recent excavations at other sites,[4] including the discovery of two important Diaspora synagogues at Ostia[5] and at Sardis,[6] have shown that the unorthodoxy which Dura exhibits is not so rare. The Dura synagogue should now be seen as one of several synagogues known both in Palestine and in the Diaspora which do not conform to the established classifications.[7] Thus the evidence from Dura takes on new significance.

From that perspective, a comparison of the Dura building with the synagogue at Sardis provides an interesting basis for a reexamination of some of the issues. In general appearance the two buildings are quite different; the contrast demonstrates the great diversity of synagogue architecture in the Roman Diaspora. Yet there are also important parallels, made more cogent because of the fundamental differences, and these suggest some conclusions which may be of importance for the history of ancient synagogues.

The Dura synagogue occupied the central portion of a block just inside the western stretch of city wall (fig. 10). Carl Kraeling describes it as "located on one of the less desirable streets of the city."[8] The quarter is "basically residential in character."[9] One private house was modified to form an earlier, smaller synagogue, while another house was converted later when the synagogue was enlarged and rebuilt. Even in its final form the Dura synagogue retained the scale of a dwelling. It was inconspicuous, and from the outside could not easily be differentiated from the neighboring houses. It was constructed in the local architectural idiom.

> The high walls and flat roof gave it a box-like appearance, quite in keeping with that of other structural units at Dura, both private dwellings and temples, but quite in contrast to that of the synagogues of Palestine.[10]

The location of the Sardis synagogue parallels Dura in that neither building was freestanding, but rather both were part of a block or complex not entirely devoted to Jewish use. Also, neither building followed the Talmudic criterion that a synagogue should occupy the highest site in town.[11] These circumstances are probably natural in densely populated cities of the Diaspora in which Jews were a small minority.

Otherwise the differences in their settings and external appearance are dramatic. The Sardis synagogue is in a prominent location, in an area that was a center of civic life, not in a secluded residential quarter. It occupies the southeast corner of a grand and monumental public building complex, a Roman bath-gymnasium, and it lies alongside a major thoroughfare of the city, a colonnaded avenue lined with shops, perhaps the successor to the Persian Royal

Road (fig. 11). The building site was originally to have
been developed as part of the pagan gymnasium.
Later that corner of the complex was turned over to
the Jewish community to use for a synagogue. The
synagogue part of the complex was rebuilt under
Jewish auspices but retained its Roman architectural
character and giant scale. In its tenure as a synagogue
it was still clearly visible as a major structure, consist-
ing (in its final form) of a great basilical hall, a peristyle forecourt, and a colonnaded porch with special
emphasis on the central axis of the building (figs. 12,
13.

Entrance to the later Dura synagogue was gained
through a suite of rooms which are part of a building
called House H (fig. 14). House H insulated the forecourt and assembly room from the street and provided considerable privacy, contrasting sharply with
the direct access from a public street into the court at
Sardis. No material evidence is given in the *Final
Report* for the use of the annex rooms at Dura, but
Kraeling concludes that one suite of rooms served as a
guest house for transients while the other suite served
as rooms for an official of the synagogue. He thinks
there might have been a kitchen in one of the open
courts (H9).[12] The *Preliminary Report* suggests
schoolrooms for children and rooms for feasts.[13]

At Sardis there are no good candidates for annex
rooms serving these activities. Conceivably, guests

might have been housed in the lofts above the shops south of the synagogue, some of which were occupied by Jewish merchants. Part of the porch of the synagogue was walled off and then used as an eating place, but this occurred toward the end of the building's occupation. There is some evidence, from an inscription, that at least one of the rooms to the west of the synagogue (room BE-A in fig. 11) was occupied by Jews for part of its history,[14] but the use of these rooms remains enigmatic. The suite of west rooms was closely connected with the rest of the complex,[15] but the only direct access from the synagogue proper was via the little chamber south of the apse, through a narrow passage rudely cut through the thick wall, probably at a late date.[16] It seems, then, that no formal provision was made for annex rooms on the site at the height of the Jewish occupation.

Beyond the annex rooms of the later Dura synagogue is a colonnaded forecourt. The court at Sardis is similar in several respects. The parallel is striking, and I will return to it later.

The innermost room at Dura, the House of Assembly, is a simple rectangular room with entrances on one long wall, a small aedicula as Torah shrine on the wall opposite, and benches along the walls all around (fig. 14). Kraeling estimates that the benches could seat at least 65 people.[17]

At Sardis, the assembly room is quite different, more nearly a typical basilical hall, symmetrical about its long axis, containing two rows of large piers (figs. 12, 13). The hall was entered through three doors on one short wall, with a large apse on the opposite end. There are no benches along the side walls as there are at Dura. At Sardis, worshippers must have stood, or sat on the floor, or used portable seats. The floors were paved with mosaics, and the lower portions of walls were revetted with marble intarsia work set within an architectonic frame. According to an inscription,[18] there were paintings on the walls (higher up) or on the ceiling, and fragments of wall or ceiling mosaic were found in the collapse. Compared with the simplicity of the hall at Dura, the Sardis hall is elaborate and ambitious. The most striking contrast is in size; the assembly hall at Sardis has about ten times the floor area as the hall at Dura, and measures ca. 54 meters from entrance wall to apse.[19]

The contrast reflects, in part at least, differences in size and wealth of the two Jewish communities and in their positions in Roman society.[20] At Sardis, the prominent location and great size of the synagogue attest a large and influential Jewish community. The inscriptions found inside reveal more explicitly the relation of the Sardis Jews to government authority: nine synagogue donors are identified as city councilors (*bouleutai*); two other men are identified as record-office functionaries in the Roman provincial administration (*boethoi taboulariou*); another was a former procurator (*apo epitropon*);[21] yet another is referred to as a count (*comes*).[22] The city maintained a cordial or at least tolerant attitude toward the Sardis Jewish community for a long time; the Jews were able to renovate the synagogue handsomely in the second half of the fourth century A.D. and once again at a later date. There is some evidence of retrenchment toward the end, but the building was in use as a synagogue until a Persian raid which destroyed much of the city in 616 A.D. According to A. T. Kraabel, the evidence reveals

> a Jewish community quite integrated into the social, economic and political life of a major Anatolian city, while retaining an internal cohesion and a clear understanding of itself as a part of Diaspora Judaism.[23]

He adds:

> Nothing in the archaeological or epigraphic evidence would suggest exclusiveness of any kind; they participate fully in the community's life.[24]

This is quite a contrast with the seclusion and introverted character of the Dura building and with Kraeling's assessment of a Judaism which

> tended to turn more and more away from the
> world and back upon itself, concerning itself
> ever more exclusively with the vast body of
> tradition its scholars and preachers had created
> for it out of their study of the sacred book.[25]

Yet there are some interesting parallels in the arrangement of the two assembly halls. One of these is that neither building had provision for worship by women in the manner traditionally ascribed to most ancient synagogues.

For the Sardis synagogue to conform to the traditional view, it should have had a separate entrance leading to a balcony or gallery for women to attend worship within the main hall. The hall had piers, which could have served to support such a balcony, but no appropriate stairs have been found and it is quite difficult to imagine how access to a balcony might have been arranged except by something like a ladder, which could hardly have been used regularly for public assembly. If there was a gallery of some kind, I doubt that it was used for women at worship. It is convenient, then, to have the analogy of the Dura synagogue, where there was no gallery at all.

In the later synagogue at Dura, according to the excavation reports, women worshipped in the same space as the men, but entered through the south door, and were segregated inside by being assigned to separate benches—those where there are no footrests in the upper row.[26] At Sardis, no evidence remains of physical means to separate men and women within the main hall. I cannot rule out a "portable and make-shift" partition such as Kraeling suggests could have further separated men and women at Dura.[27] However, it is hard to see where such a partition would effectively have been located in either building.[28]

To further complicate the issue, even the interpretation of the benches of the later building at Dura is open to question. I say that because in the earlier Dura synagogue, too, some of the benches have foot-rests while others do not (fig. 15), but the distribution of the two bench types in the earlier building was such that a different explanation was needed. Kraeling writes of the earlier arrangement:

> The distinction is not determined in this instance by the sex of the persons for whom they were intended. Rather it would seem that the foot-rests serve to make up for inequalities in the height of the benches.[29]

Kraeling surmises that in the earlier synagogue at Dura women were not admitted to the assembly room (room 2) but sat outside in an adjoining chamber (room 7).[30] He argues that this arrangement reflects "a conservative attitude"[31] while in the later synagogue "the arrangement is more liberal than that known from the synagogues of Palestine."[32] The architectural evidence does not clearly support this distinction[33] nor does it indicate which interpretation would best apply to Sardis. It seems best for now to conclude only that without a gallery there seem to be three general possibilities: 1) women were allowed in the assembly hall with men, though possibly in a separate part of the hall, 2) women were admitted only as far as the court or an adjoining room, 3) women were excluded from the synagogue entirely.[34]

The question of provision for women at worship which Dura and Sardis raises should extend also to other ancient synagogues, including those of the Galilean type. The assumption that these buildings had balconies for women is based largely on interpretations of literature; supporting architectural evidence is rare.[35] I was surprised to discover that no staircases are shown in most of the published plans.[36] Whatever is true about the Galilean buildings, Dura and Sardis indicate that women's galleries were not universal in ancient synagogues; perhaps they were not even typical. The architectural evidence concerning galleries in synagogues should be reexamined.

Though the hall at Sardis had no benches and apparently no gallery, it did contain several other furnishings. These are best discussed in connection with the question of the direction of focus of worship.

At Dura, the Torah niche is on the wall nearest

Jerusalem. This arrangement allowed worshippers to face the niche with its Scrolls and to face Jerusalem simultaneously (approximately, but not exactly).[37] At Sardis, the orientation of the building with respect to Jerusalem at first appears to be the reverse of that at Dura; that is, as you enter and face the apse you look *away* from Jerusalem. But the apse at Sardis in its final form does not seem to have been a receptacle for the Ark;[38] rather it contains three tiers of concentric benches which probably served as seats for the elders.[39] The Scrolls were probably kept in one of the two aedicular shrines built against the entrance wall on the Jerusalem end of the hall (shown restored in fig. 13).[40]

The matter of orientation is conventionally explained in the following way. Early synagogues, such as those of the Galilean type, were built with their entrances in the Jerusalem-oriented wall, and prayers were said facing the openings of the facades (the Scrolls of the Law were portable, and were brought out at appropriate times in the worship service). Later it became customary to build a permanent repository for the Scrolls, and so synagogues were built with an apse or niche in the Jerusalem wall while the doors were placed at the opposite end. We saw this later arrangement at a relatively early date at Dura. The theory adds that to accommodate this change of practice in synagogues that were already existing, a place for the Torah was built on the entrance wall. This "transitional solution" has been noted at Ostia and Beth She'arim, and it seems to apply at Sardis as well.[41]

However, there are several ancient synagogues which do not conform to those rules.[42] That, plus the presence at Sardis of the apse with its benches at the end away from Jerusalem suggest that the rules are oversimplified, that the matter of orientation is more complex. At Sardis, there seems to have been a multiple focus.

There was a great marble table (with eagles carved on its supports) set up in the first bay in front of the apse, and there were freestanding sculpted lions nearby, probably flanking the table (figs. 12, 13, the lions have not yet been reinstalled).[43] That group of furnishings emphasizes the westward direction, away from Jerusalem.

In the very center of the hall, four marble slabs set into the floor supported a lightweight structure, perhaps a reader's platform (bema).[44] This feature seems to provide yet another focus.

Not all of the furnishings were installed at the same time. Nevertheless, they seem to have coexisted for a while. The hall probably had multiple uses, perhaps including several of the functions which at Dura occured in the annex rooms, and the several focuses could have been associated with the different activities. Perhaps worshippers at prayer faced the shrines at the east end of the hall, whereas readings and discourses were delivered from the bema in the center, where the reader could be heard by the greatest number. The west end with its benches conceivably functioned as a tribunal.[45] Kraabel points to a mosaic inscription, prominently placed among the bema stones in the center of the hall, which mentions a teacher *(sophodidaskalos)*; he suggests that a school was part of this complex, and thought that the most likely location for classes would be the main hall itself. He adds that the hall might have been used as a sort of community building, for social and even political gatherings.[46] Whatever the uses of the hall, the inconsistency of the direction of the mosaic inscriptions indicates that there was some ambiguity about orientation; some of the inscriptions are read facing east, while others face west.[47]

In discussing orientation, it is important to note that both buildings were remodeled several times, and in both cases the final plans were strongly dependent on the earlier development on the site. Both synagogues were originally created by renovating a structure built for a different, secular purpose, and in both cases the boundaries which had been established for the original building had great influence on the final synagogue form. The sequences show the degree to which the building programs could be accommodated and perhaps even subordinated to the characteristics of the site.

The earlier synagogue at Dura was adapted from a private dwelling. In the rebuilding of 245 A.D., the forecourt and prayer hall were enlarged and an adjacent house was taken over for the new annex rooms (cf. figs. 14, 15).[48]

At Sardis, excavations show a history of four major stages (fig. 16).[49] The foundations were laid out after 17 A.D. for three rooms associated with the gymnasium palaestra (stage 1). Then, apparently before the first plan was completed, the building was converted to a basilical hall with a small vestibule (stage 2). The third stage is the least clear, but the dating of inscriptions indicates that the building was in use as a synagogue by the third century A.D., yet at a time before the present forecourt was built. The court was created in a fourth stage of construction which is dated to the second half of the fourth century A.D.

Note that the final renovation at both Sardis and Dura involved the creation of a colonnaded court on the central axis. The courtyard of the earlier synagogue at Dura was smaller and off to one side, and the earlier stage at Sardis does not seem to have included a court at all. In both cases the renovation was done under Jewish auspices.

Several other ancient synagogues have courtyards,

too. Not enough attention has been paid to their functions, their origins and development, or their relation to the atriums of Christian churches.

At both Dura and Sardis, the forecourts contained a water source; at Dura a small facility in the northwest corner;[50] at Sardis an elaborate waterworks with a fountain in the form of a marble urn in the center of the court[51] and also a smaller marble basin to the south (perhaps a later addition). The courts at Dura and Sardis probably served for the washing of hands before prayer[52] in addition to functioning in a general way as ante-rooms or gathering places for entry into the assembly halls.[53]

Other uses for synagogue courts have been discussed also. Some writers suggest that they were used as lodging for strangers.[54] Kraeling writes:

> Here questions of common importance were discussed, here public announcements were made, here scholars studied and debated the interpretation of the Law, and here, no doubt, children were instructed.[55]

Kraeling distinguishes two periods in the history of courtyards in ancient synagogues. He argues that in Galilean synagogues of the Antonine and Severan periods the peristyle is usually at the side, while in later synagogues "the tendency is to transfer the colonnaded courtyard to the front of the building."[56]

Two modifications of this theory are necessary. First, courtyards may not have been typical in synagogues of the Galilean type. Their existence has often been assumed by analogy with the synagogue at Capernaum, where the court is well preserved. However, courtyards are not shown in the plans of other Galilean synagogues in the study by Kohl and Watzinger.[57] Moreover, the dating of Capernaum is now in dispute, with some recent scholarship suggesting a fourth century date.[58] The Dura synagogue may be among the earliest with courtyards.

Second, more is involved than merely the side of the building the court is on. At Dura and at Sardis, the courts built in the final reconstruction are carefully placed so as to lie symmetrically about the center axis of the building. I interpret this as a deliberately desired relationship, not an incidental one.[59] A detail demonstrates the importance attached to the position and formal organization of the courts at Dura and Sardis: in both buildings the side doors to the assembly halls are placed comfortably with respect to the side porches of the courtyard, but awkwardly with respect to features in the inner room.[60] Not all later synagogues have courtyards, and some have courts at the side.[61] But axial courts such as we see most clearly at Dura and Sardis occur also in the synagogues at Beth Alpha, Jerash, Miletus (if it was a synagogue), Priene, and nearly so at Stobi.[62]

The development of axial forecourts, which create formal settings for the assembly hall and the forecourt activities, may be associated with the introduction of a place for the Torah Scrolls in a position of prominence and honor on the Jerusalem wall. Both features seem to represent attempts to provide differentiated, specialized settings for the activities associated with them. The two developments seem to occur at roughly the same time (possibly first at Dura in both cases), and both are associated with an articulation and extension of the central axis. They may represent a new or increased emphasis on the directionality of worship, or at least a stronger architectural expression of it.

Contrasting with the synagogues in which axiality is so developed are the buildings of the Galilean type, which do not have strong directional thrust, in which the colonnade typically continues around three sides of the hall, and in which, though there is some emphasis on the entrance wall, attention is largely directed inward to the central space.[63]

I propose, then, that to the list of features which identify the "later" or "Byzantine type" of synagogue we should add as a distinguishing, though not universal, characteristic the frontal court and the strengthening of architectural directionality that it helps produce.

Seen in this light, the synagogue at

Dura-Europos appears as an early and important step in the development of the later type of synagogue, though in the broadhouse arrangement and with the benches on four walls it retains some of the inward focussing of the earlier, simpler buildings.[64] At Sardis, the axis is strongly developed architecturally, but worship was not directed at the apse as would normally be expected, in part at least because of the constraints of the prior building. Elsewhere, most clearly at Beth Alpha, the architectural arrangement comes in harmony with the liturgical direction.

It is curious that we have seen the axial development in two Diaspora synagogues, Sardis and Dura, which are otherwise quite different architecturally; they differ in size, in setting, in details of construction—each built in its regional architectural idiom—in the provision of annex rooms, and in the arrangement of furnishings in the assembly hall. The latter suggests that the assembly halls must have functioned rather differently.[65] The two synagogues are also quite far apart geographically, and this raises the question of the origins of the axial plan.

Carl Kraeling argues that the aedicula at Dura is derived from contemporary Mesopotamian religious architecture.[66] Emphasizing the aedicula as "the fundamental element in the development of a synagogue architecture," he suggests "that Babylonia rather than Palestine should be regarded as the pioneer in, and the most significant contributor to, the development of the synagogue as a formal structure."[67]

Kraeling sees the court as an independent development with humbler origins. The courtyard at Dura, he argues, is derived from a modification of local domestic architecture.[68]

Mesopotamian influence on the plans and aedicula of the Dura synagogue and on the development of ancient synagogue architecture in general should certainly be explored further, but the colonnaded court as part of the "formal plan" would seem to have its origins in the West, with its roots in Hellenistic-Roman monumental building rather than in Mesopotamian domestic architecture.[69] Sardis was a major Roman city, and Dura had been under Roman control for almost a century when the second synagogue with its axial court was built. Kraeling observes that by the time of the remodelling,

> a new element brought up in a more Hellenized environment had joined the community, had helped to swell its ranks, and had gained in the group a position of some influence and dignity.[70]

This new element might have been responsible for the renovation.

Finally, the development of the formal plan

brings me to the relationship of these synagogues to
Early Christian architecture, and of Judaism to Early
Christianity. I will only raise the issue again in a new
light.

Kraeling notes that the shift in position of the
peristyle court "has the effect of creating in synagogue architecture a counterpart to the atrium of the
Christian basilica." But he concludes that the development of frontal peristyle courts and axial apses in
both Jewish and Christian buildings "are analogous
but not apparently directly interrelated."[71] I am not
so sure. The basilican hall with a nave and aisles plus
an apse (or two) was used for public assembly of
many types in the Roman world, but both Christianity and Judaism appear to have fused the hall and a
frontal court in similar fashion at about the same
time. This, plus the startling resemblance of the
Sardis synagogue to some early church plans, ought
to provide good material for a reevaluation of the
theological as well as the architectural relationships.

*This paper is an outgrowth of my work since 1966 as architect for the restoration and forthcoming final publication of the Sardis synagogue. I am grateful to the directors of the Sardis Expedition, G. M. A. Hanfmann, the late A. H. Detweiler, and S. W. Jacobs, for the opportunity to participate as a member of the expedition staff. My participation in the field work and as Research Fellow for Sardis in the Fogg Art Museum, Harvard University, was made possible by grants to the expedition from the National Endowment for the Humanities (grant numbers H 67-0-56, H 68-0-61, H 69-0-23, RO-111-70-3966, RO-4999-71-171, and RO-6435-72-264) and by vital aid from the Memorial Foundation for Jewish Culture, the Supporters of Sardis, and the Committee to Preserve the Ancient Synagogue of Sardis. I am indebted also to D. L. Moe, of the Harvard Divinity School, as the arguments presented here were much sharpened through conversations with him.

1. Carl H. Kraeling, *The Excavations at Dura-Europos, Final Report* VIII, part 1: *The Synagogue*, eds. A. R. Bellinger, F. E. Brown, A. Perkins, C. B. Welles (New Haven, 1956), 3-33, 255-260 concern the architecture and furnishings; of particular interest for the discussions in this paper are the sections "Synagogue Forecourts, Their Functions and Origin" (p. 13), "Synagogue Types and Structural Principles" (pp. 20-25), "The House Synagogue" (pp. 32-33). Also H. F. Pearson and C. H. Kraeling, "The Synagogue," *The Excavations at Dura-Europos, Preliminary Report of the Sixth Season of Work*, eds. M. I. Rostovtzeff, A. R. Bellinger, C. Hopkins, C. B. Welles (New Haven, 1936), 309-396. See especially section I, "History and Architecture," by H. R. Pearson, 309-337. A brief account of the buildings is given by M. I. Rostovtzeff, *Dura-Europos and its Art* (Oxford, 1938), 61-62, 100-130. The monumental series by E. R. Goodenough, *Jewish Symbols in the Greco-Roman Period* (New York, 1953-1968), treats the evidence from Dura extensively, though generally dealing with the wall paintings. He discusses the architecture in vols. I (1953), 227-232; IX (1964), 15-16, 25-37; X (1964), 197-198; XII (1965), 158-160; with plates in vol. XI.

2. Carl H. Kraeling, "The Earliest Synagogue Architecture," *BASOR* 54 (1934), 18-20, noted shortly after the building was discovered: "The interior has not the slightest resemblance to a basilica and lacks entirely the parallel rows of superimposed columns and the gallery and peaked roof which is found in Palestinian synagogues." He further compares the Dura synagogue with synagogues of the Galilean type in *Final Report* (supra n. 1), 13, 14, 21, 23-25, 32. Identification of the Galilean type was established by Heinrich Kohl and Carl Watzinger, *Antike Synagogen in Galilaea* (Leipzig, 1916), and is basic to subsequent surveys of ancient synagogue development. Especially notable surveys are:

𝔰ꝗ0𝔰5

E. L. Sukenik, *Ancient Synagogues in Palestine and Greece* (London, 1934); Goodenough (supra n. 1), I 178-267, II 70-100; and a very useful article by M. Avi-Yonah, "Synagogue Architecture in the Classical Period, " *Jewish Art, An Illustrated History*, ed. Cecil Roth (New York, 1961), cols. 155-190. Cf. also J. Gutmann, "The Origin of the Synagogue: The Current State of Research," *Archäologischer Anzeiger* 87 (1972), 36-40. Generalizations are often made about ancient synagogues from the evidence found in Galilee, under the assumption that the Galilean type is normative of "early" synagogues even in the Diaspora. That view may be implicit in some conclusions about synagogue development presented in this paper, yet there seems to be little archaeological basis for it. The Galilean type (as the name suggests) may be a localized rather than a universal form.

3. Identification of the Byzantine type also goes back to the work of Kohl and Watzinger, summarized by Watzinger in *Denkmäler Palästinas, Eine Einführung in die Archäologie des heiligen Landes* II (Leipzig, 1935), 114-116. Avi-Yonah (supra n. 2), cols. 179-187, uses the term "later type" and gives as its characteristics: a basilical plan with two rows of columns or pillars but no transverse colonnade, an apse on the Jerusalem wall with a raised floor, entrance usually by three doors in the wall opposite the apse, mosaic pavements, women's galleries, and relatively flimsy construction compared with the earlier synagogues. Generally similar though vaguer classifications which correspond broadly to Avi-Yonah's "later type" are given by Sukenik, *Ancient Synagogues* (supra n. 2), 27-28, and Goodenough (supra n. 1), I, 238-264 ("Synagogues with Mosaics"), with introductory comments on pp. 225-226. Avi-Yonah interposes a "transitional" class of synagogues between the

"Galilean type" and the "later type" (cols. 173-179). He places the Dura synagogue in this transitional category, a period of experimentation dated to the third through sixth centuries A.D. Goodenough also places Dura in a third classification which he calls the "broadhouse type" (I, 225-237) and which he seems to regard as an intermediate category.

4. Much of the recent work is included in S. J. Saller, *A Revised Catalogue of the Ancient Synagogues of the Holy Land* (Jerusalem, 1969), a convenient compilation with a brief summary and bibliography for each site.

5. M. F. Squarciapino, "The Synagogue at Ostia," tr. by Lionel Casson, *Archaeology* 16 (1963), 194-203; M. F. Squarciapino, "La Sinagoga di Ostia: seconda campagna di scavo," *Atti del VI Congresso Internazionale di Archaeologia Cristiana* (Ravenna, 23-29 settembre 1962), 299-315; M. F. Squarciapino, "La sinagoga di Ostia," *Bolletino d'arte* 4 (1961), 326-337. A brief account, small plan, and two photographs are given in Rachel Wischnitzer, *The Architecture of the European Synagogue* (Philadelphia, 1964), 5-7, figs. 3-5.

6. There is ample documentary evidence for the existence of a Jewish community at Sardis, but (for Sardis as was true of Dura) nothing was known of the building itself until the excavation of the physical remains. The building was discovered in 1962. Preliminary reports have been published annually in *BASOR* 170 (1963), 38-48; 174 (1964), 30-44; 177 (1965), 17-21; 182 (1966), 34-45; 187 (1967), 9-50, 60-62; 191 (1968), 26-32; 199 (1970), 45-53; 203 (1971), 12-18; 206 (1972), 20-23, 33-39. Also G. M. A. Hanfmann, "The Ancient Synagogue of Sardis," *Fourth World Congress of Jewish*

Studies, Papers I (1967), 37-42; D. G. Mitten, "A New Look at Ancient Sardis," *BiblArch* 29 (1966), 61-67; A. R. Seager, "The Building History of the Sardis Synagogue," *AJA* 76 (1972), 425-435, pls. 91-94. On Judaism at Sardis and the use of the synagogue and its furnishings: E. R. Goodenough (supra n. 1), XII, 191-195; A. T. Kraabel, "Judaism in Western Asia Minor under the Roman Empire, with a Preliminary Study of the Jewish Community at Sardis, Lydia" (Ph.D. Thesis, Harvard Divinity School, March 1968), 198-249, forthcoming in the series *Studia Post-Biblica* (Leiden). See also A. T. Kraabel, "*Hypsistos* and the Synagogue at Sardis," *Greek, Roman and Byzantine Studies* 10 (1969), 81-93; G. M. A. Hanfmann and Jane C. Waldbaum, "New Excavations at Sardis and Some Problems of Western Anatolian Archaeology," *Near Eastern Archaeology in the Twentieth Century*, Essays in Honor of Nelson Glueck, ed. J. A. Sanders (New York, 1970), 317-320; Y. Shiloh, "Torah Scrolls and the Menorah Plaque from Sardis," *Israel Exploration Journal* 18:1 (1968), 54-57, pls. 4A, 4B; A. T. Kraabel, "Melito the Bishop and the Synagogue at Sardis: Text and Context," *Studies Presented to George M. A. Hanfmann*, eds. D. G. Mitten, J. G. Pedley, J. A. Scott, Fogg Art Museum Monographs in Art and Archaeology II (Cambridge, Mass. and Mainz, 1971), 77-85. Final publication of the Sardis synagogue is in preparation.

7. In addition to Ostia and Sardis, a list would include the synagogues in Avi-Yonah's transitional category (see n. 3 above) plus the recently discovered synagogue at Khirbet Shemaᶜ, reported by Eric Meyers, A. Thomas Kraabel, James Strange, "Archaeology and Rabbinic Tradition at Khirbet Shemaᶜ, 1970 and 1971 Campaigns," *BiblArch* 35 (1972), 1-31. See also n. 42 below.

8. Kraeling, *Final Report* (supra n. 1), 328.

9. *Ibid.*, 3.

10. *Ibid.*, 14.

11. The prescription was ignored often. Kraeling, *ibid.*, 23, nn. 104-105, notes this Talmudic canon and points out that it would have been difficult to observe in the "relatively flat terrain" of Dura. The siting of synagogues is discussed briefly by Sukenik, *Ancient Synagogues* (supra n. 2), 49-50, and Avi-Yonah (supra n. 2), cols. 159-160, who mention an alternative of building synagogues in the proximity of water, though no official precept to that effect is preserved.

12. Kraeling, *Final Report* (supra n. 1), 7-11.

13. Pearson (supra n. 1), 312. Sukenik, *Ancient Synagogues* (supra n. 2), 48-49, says of ancient synagogues generally, "The functions of the annexes may be taken with some certainty to have been those of classrooms for children and guest rooms for strangers."

14. The inscription is IN64.1. See the preliminary report on the "Synagogue Annex" *BASOR* 187 (1967), 10-21.

15. Room BE-C still contained at the time of its destruction an inscribed marble base (IN72.1) recording a dedication under the co-emperors Caracalla and Geta of statues of the children of the goddess Kore.

16. *BASOR* 187 (1967), 18, fig. 42.

17. Kraeling, *Final Report* (supra n. 1), 334.

18. By the husband of Regina, No. 7 in L. Robert, *Nouvellès inscriptions de Sardes* (Paris, 1964), 48-54. Also Hanfmann, "The Ancient Synagogue of Sardis" (supra n. 6), 39. For other donations inscriptions, see n. 21.

19. Goodenough (supra n. 1), XII 191, 193, finds the Sardis synagogue analogous to the description in the Talmud of the Hellenistic *diplostoon* of the Jews in Alexandria, destroyed in 116 A.D. (translations of the text are conveniently given by Goodenough, II, 85f., and by Avi-Yonah [supra n. 2], cols. 157-158). The parallel raises the speculation that there might be other basilican synagogues on the scale of the Sardis building but of even earlier date, perhaps deriving from the great Alexandrian building, but of which (like the Sardis synagogue) no written accounts are preserved.

20. It is important to note that there was more than a century between the construction of the second synagogue at Dura, 245 A.D., and the final major renovation at Sardis, in the second half of the fourth century. The time interval may be responsible for some of the differences between the two buildings. However, evidence exists that there was an earlier synagogue on the same site at Sardis at a time roughly contemporary with the second synagogue at Dura. While this earlier phase differed in some important respects from the final plan, it already occupied roughly the same large area, was already in the form of a great basilical hall, and already served a large and powerful Jewish community. For details, see Seager (supra n. 6), 432-434.

21. These are noted in the conclusion of a report on the inscriptions by G. M. A. Hanfmann, *BASOR* 187 (1967), 27-32, which is based on a study by J. H. Kroll with the help of comments by L. Robert, "The Synagogue Dona-

tions Inscriptions, Report, 1966" (Sardis Expedition files, unpublished). According to Kraabel, "Judaism" (supra n. 6), 219-220, "The city councilors (*bouleutai*) would be men of substance, economic and social powers as well as political leaders ... The procurator in particular, as an imperial agent, would have been a powerful man, able to reach the ear of higher provincial officials." Inscriptions in floor mosaics and on plaques of marble revetment found the first year of excavation are published by L. Robert (supra n. 18), 37-58. Mosaic inscriptions found the first year are also reported in *BASOR* 170 (1963), 41-42, 46-48, fig. 32. For mosaic inscriptions found in subsequent seasons, *BASOR* 174 (1964), 30-33, fig. 17; *BASOR* 187 (1967), 29, 32-46, figs. 46-56; *BASOR* 206 (1972), 20.

22. IN71.15. See *BASOR* 206 (1972), 20.

23. Kraabel, "Judaism" (supra n. 6), 9-10.

24. *Ibid.*, 245.

25. Kraeling, *Final Report* (supra n. 1), 325. Cf. Goodenough (supra n. 1), X 206, where he disagrees.

26. Kraeling, *Final Report* (supra n. 1), 16, 23-24; Pearson (supra n. 1), 323-324.

27. Kraeling, *Final Report* (supra n. 1), 24, n. 110.

28. As noted about the Dura arrangement by Pearson (supra n. 1), 323.

29. Kraeling, *Final Report* (supra n. 1), 30.

30. *Ibid.*, 32; similarly on p. 31.

31. *Ibid.*, 32.

32. *Ibid.*, 24.

33. Goodenough (supra n. 1) is skeptical of Kraeling's interpretations. Regarding the earlier synagogue, he notes
(IX, 30-31) that "the well-worn threshold of the little
door that joined Room 7 with Room 2 indicates a frequency of going back and forth unthinkable if the room
was used for women," and suggests instead that room 7
had a "cultic relation" to room 2. In challenging
Kraeling's interpretation of the benches in the later synagogue, he argues that the principle of separating the
sexes at Jewish worship "antedates all surviving synagogues" and he supposes that where no balcony was
provided for women "they stood outside, in an open
court, or in the open air, or . . . ordinarily did not themselves go to the synagogues at all" (I, 226; also I, 204
and I, 210, n. 250). He also (I, 228) cites E. L. Sukenik,
The Ancient Synagogue of El-Hammeh (Jerusalem,
1953), 73: "The possibility must also be admitted that
no provision was made at all for women worshippers in
the synagogue of Dura-Europos; for women are by
Jewish law exempt from the duty of prayer. Individual
women desirous of participating in divine services could
follow them from the court, or possibly from a pew
reserved for them inside."

34. These alternatives are basically those listed by Pearson
(supra n. 1), 337.

35. Sukenik gives an argument in favor of women's galleries
in *Ancient Synagogues* (supra n. 2), 47-48, but it does
not seem to warrant the sureness with which he states
(p. 22) that at Chorazin there was "a staircase, which of
course mounted to the women's gallery." He gives

further evidence in *El-Hammeh* (supra n. 33), 72-73:
"An internal staircase may still be seen at the synagogue
of Chorazin, at the northern end of the annex on its
west side, and it seems there was also one at Beth Alpha
in the annex at the southwest end of the basilica." But
this still does not seem sufficient for the conclusion that
"in Palestine . . . most synagogue ruins have preserved
unmistakeable traces of a gallery." Avi-Yonah (supra n.
2), cols. 163-164, says of the Galilean synagogues that
"we have to assume the existence of a gallery resting on
the columns running around three sides," and he cites
architectural evidence which consists of "steps actually
found, as at Capernaum," columns in the debris smaller
than those of the main colonnade, and the finding of
screen slabs. Even if galleries were common in ancient
synagogues (but see n. 36 below), this alone does not
mean conclusively that their purpose was to provide for
women at worship. Cf. S. Safrai, "Was there a Women's
Gallery in the Synagogue of Antiquity?" *Tarbiz* 22
(1963), 329-38 (Hebrew with English summary, p. II).

36.   Kohl and Watzinger (supra n. 2), pls. II, VII-VIII, X-XII,
      XIV-XVII, show plans of ten Galilean synagogues. Stairs
      appropriate for a gallery are indicated only at
      Capernaum (pl. II) and with a question mark in the res-
      toration plan (though not the excavation plan) at Kefr
      Bir'im (pl. XII).

37.   Discussed in Kraeling, *Final Report* (supra n. 1), 24-25.

38.   The apse was originally built with three niches and two
      diagonal passages, but these were later walled shut. In its
      final form, with a patterned mosaic floor but without
      niches in its wall surface, the apse has no appropriate
      accommodation for an Ark.

39. Nothing in the preserved state of the benches indicated that one seat was more prominent or more distinguished than the others, such as was the case with the "Elder's Seat" at Dura (cf. Kraeling, *Final Report* [supra n. 1], 17, 260).

40. The one shrine column complete at the top has a small dowel hole which could have held hardware for a curtain or veil (cf. the veil at Dura, Kraeling, *Final Report* [supra n. 1), 257-259).

41. Cf. the explanations of orientation given by Sukenik, *Ancient Synagogues* (supra n. 2), 27, 50-53; Kraeling, *Final Report* (supra n. 1), 24-25; Goodenough (supra n. 1), I, 209-210, 226, 239; Avi-Yonah (supra n. 2), cols. 171-174, 179-180; Wischnitzer (supra n. 5), 5-7, 13-15; Kraabel, "Judaism" (supra n. 6), 231. For a rather different view of orientation, Franz Landsberger, "The Sacred Direction in Synagogue and Church," *HUCA* 28 (1957), 181-203.

42. D. L. Moe kindly made available to me his 1972 prospectus for a doctoral dissertation at the Harvard Divinity School, "Capernaum and Ancient Synagogues," in which he lists the synagogues at Isfiya, Khirbet Semmâka, Yafa, ed-Dikke, Umm el-Kanâtir, Hulda, Naʿaran, Herodium, Masada, and Beth Sheʿan as not conforming to the traditional view of orientation (pp. 17-35).

43. *BASOR* 174 (1964), 34-36, 38, figs. 19, 23. Goodenough (supra n. 1), XII 195, fig. 4. The table was in place, though broken, when found. The lions were shattered, with fragments scattered around the table.

44. *BASOR* 182 (1966), 44-45, fig. 35. The slabs are instru-

sions in the mosaic and may have been added later than the table. The *diplostoon* at Alexandria also had a central bema, of wood, according to the Talmudic description (see n. 19 above).

45. Suggested by Kraabel, "Judaism" (supra n. 6), 226. Goodenough (supra n. 1), XII, 195, excited by the discovery of the table, suspected "that the west end with the apse and table at Sardis was screened off, and that the table was indeed the center of ritual for those who sat on the benches." However, while there is evidence for a screen along the west face of the apse, there is no evidence at all for a screen on the east side of the table.

46. Kraabel, "Judaism" (supra n. 6), 226. The inscription is IN66.3; see *BASOR* 187 (1967), 29, 38, fig. 48. Goodenough (supra n. 1), XII, 191, suggests that the main hall functioned also as a place "where men of various crafts worked and sold their goods," on analogy with the great Alexandrian *diplostoon*, but Kraabel (p. 238) thinks this unlikely because of the presence of shops nearby.

47. See *BASOR* 170 (1963), 47; 187 (1967), 29; also n. 21 above.

48. For details see Kraeling, *Final Report* (supra n. 1), 26-33. Concerning the published reconstruction plan of the earlier building, I only note that the nearly square patch in the center of the assembly room floor which marks the location of an object later removed (apparently while the earlier synagogue was still in use), and which Avi-Yonah (supra n. 2), cols. 176-177, thinks indicates the presence of a bema there, occupies the position analogous to the bema at Sardis.

49. These are detailed in Seager (supra n. 6), 430-435.

50. Kraeling, *Final Report* (supra n. 1), 13, 28.

51. *BASOR* 191 (1968), 29-31, fig. 23; also *BASOR* 170 (1963), 46-47.

52. Kraeling, *Final Report* (supra n. 1), 13, says this of Dura. According to Sukenik, *Ancient Synagogues* (supra n. 2), 49, this is the normal function of synagogue courts: "A courtyard, which might be situated on any side of the synagogue, contained vessels with water for the washing of hands before prayer."

53. Kraeling, *Final Report* (supra n. 1), 12, says that at Dura the court provided "a fitting transition to, and setting for, the magnificence of the innermost chamber." Avi-Yonah (supra n. 2), col. 163, also notes this function as an ante-room. Goodenough (supra n. 1), I, 182, suggests that the court served for worshippers who were not admitted to the inner room, which may have been accessible only to a select group.

54. Goodenough (supra n. 1), I, 182; Avi-Yonah (supra n. 2), col. 163.

55. Kraeling, *Final Report* (supra n. 1), 13.

56. *Loc. cit.*

57. Kohl and Watzinger (supra n. 2), pls. II, VII-VIII, X-XII, XIV-XVII. Kraeling, *Final Report* (supra n. 1), n. 46 on p. 13, cites the Kohl and Watzinger plates and notes that "in all but the first the existence of such courts in inferred from the presence of side entrances to the House of Assembly." That inference is generally accepted. Thus Avi-Yonah (supra n. 2), col. 163, writes, "The court is, in fact, an almost invariable feature of these syna-

gogues." And Sukenik, *Ancient Synagogues* (supra n. 2),
22, says of Chorazin, "There was very probably a court
on the east side" (but he cites no evidence).

58. The arguments are summarized by Moe (supra n. 42),
7-9, nn. 22-28. He cites as a major source of new inform-
ation the work of Virgilio Corbo, Stanislaus Loffreda,
Augusto Spijkerman, *La Sinagoga di Cafarnao, dopo gli
scavi del 1969* (Jerusalem: Franciscan Printing Press 1970;
Collectio Minor n. 9).

59. This is not a common interpretation. Kraeling suggests
casual, circumstantial motivations behind the frontal
relationship. He argued at one time, in "The Earliest
Synagogue Architecture" (supra n. 2), 19, that in early
synagogues courts were on the side to avoid disturbing
the Jerusalem-oriented facades, but that this was no
longer necessary when it became the practice to orient
the buildings the other way around. He later wrote, in
Final Report (supra n. 1), n. 91 on p. 21, that the
frontal court "provided a way of escape from the expensive architectural and decorative embellishment of the
basilical facade." The shift in position of the court at
Dura. is attributed by Pearson, *Preliminary Report* (supra
n. 1), 314, partly to "plot limitations." Goodenough
(supra n. 1), I, 210 (and a similar sentiment on p. 226)
argues, "At Dura, when a synagogue was being constructed as best one could by tearing down partitions in
a city house, the only place the facade could be put was
out in the court." In listing characteristics of the "later"
synagogue type, Avi-Yonah (supra n. 2), cols. 179-187,
discusses courts in several places and notes the recur-
rence of a well in the center of the court, but he does
not mention the axial position.

60. Also, the courtyard sides of the door frames are more

elaborately treated than the assembly hall sides, which are simple reveals. When a comparison is made between courtyards of synagogues and atriums of early churches, it should be noted that the courts at Dura and Sardis (and in some other synagogues too) occupy the same width as the assembly halls.

61. The court of the synagogue at Na'aran, for example, is irregular in shape and extends around the side. Note, though, that on the central axis there is a separate small rectangular enclosure containing a square basin (which had a little fountain or ornamental aedicula) in pl. 5 ("plan restauré") of L. H. Vincent, "Un sanctuaire dans la région de Jericho; la synagogue de Na'arah," and Pierre Benoit, "Note additionelle," *Revue Biblique* 68 (1961), 161-173, 174-177, pls. 4-5. The synagogue of Na' aran is discussed briefly in Sukenik, *Ancient Synagogues* (supra n. 2), 28-31, figs. 4-5; and Goodenough (supra n. 1), I, 252; III, fig. 645.

62. On Beth Alpha: E. L. Sukenik, *The Ancient Synagogue of Beth Alpha* (Jerusalem, 1932). On Jerash: C. H. Kraeling, *Gerasa, City of the Decapolis* (New Haven, 1938), 236-239, 318-324, 473, plan XXXVI. On Miletus: A. von Gerkan, *Milet* I, 6, ed. T. Wiegand (Berlin, 1922), 80-82, Abb. 19, Tafel I.2 and XI. On Priene: T. Wiegand and H. Schrader, *Priene: Ergebnisse der Ausgrabungen und Untersuchungen in den Jahren 1895-1898* (Berlin, 1904), 320, 480f. Plans and brief discussion of the above are available conveniently in Sukenik, *Ancient Synagogues* (supra n. 2), 31-37, 40-43, figs. 7-9, 11, 12; and Goodenough (supra n. 1), I, 241; II, 77, 78; III, figs. 631, 641, 878-880, 882. On Stobi: Wischnitzer (supra n. 5), 7-9, fig. 6, gives a brief summary and cites J. Petrovic, "The Excavations in Stobi," *Starinar* (in Serbian), third series, VII (1932), 81-86. Cf.

M. Hengel, "Die Synagogeninschrift von Stobi,"
Zeitschrift für die Neutestamentliche Wissenschaft 57
(1966), 145-83. Kraeling, *Final Report* (supra n. 1), n.
47 on p. 13, cites Beth She'arim (along with Jerash and
Beth Alpha) as a synagogue with a frontal courtyard,
though its court is not closely parallel with the others;
see Benjamin Mazar, *Beth She'arim, Report on the Excavations during 1936-40*, vol. I: *The Catacombs I-IV*
(Jerusalem, 1957), VI-VII, 22-26. The plan is repro-
duced in Goodenough (supra n. 1), III, fig. 535. For
other sources on the Palestinian synagogues in this list,
see Saller (supra n. 4), nos. 15, 41, 100.

63.   As would be true of peristyle courts. Avi-Yonah (supra
       n. 2), col. 163, calculates that the average proportions of
       synagogues of the Galilean type are 11:10, "i.e., they are
       almost square in plan." In col. 157 he discusses the
       inward focus of Jewish prayer in synagogues, and in col.
       167 argues that interiors of Galilean synagogues were
       deliberately plain so that attention was kept con-
       centrated on prayer.

64.   Kraeling, *Final Report* (supra n. 1), 32-33, interprets the
       evidence differently. He recognizes the introduction of
       the Torah shrine as a "formal principle" (the definition
       is clearest in n. 153 but see also p. 25) and he notes that
       in Palestine (at the time that the earlier Dura synagogue
       was built) "the formal principle was not yet being
       employed." However, he does not consider the court-
       yard as part of the development of the formal plan, and
       so he argues (p. 32), "We are dealing with the same type
       of synagogue building in both levels. Since the type is a
       simple adaptation of domestic architecture, it is more
       primitive fundamentally than the type of the Galilee
       synagogues." That conclusion is not generally accepted,
       e.g. Goodenough (supra n. 1), I, 210, 226; and
       Avi-Yonah (supra n. 2), cols. 176-177, who places Dura

in a class of synagogues transitional between the "Galilean type" and the "late type."

65. Goodenough (supra n. 1), I, 3-58, argues (in trying to explain the rapid hellenization of early Christianity) that rabbinism was not of great influence in the Roman Diaspora, and that for Diaspora Jews without organized discipline the meaning and interpretation of traditional practices must have been "modified through the ages and under the influence of foreign ideas" (p. 40). The contrast between the Sardis and Dura buildings reinforces the view that Judaism in late Roman and early Byzantine times was not monolithic, but the architectural evidence is not sufficient to define these practices nor to determine whether some were of the mystical variety that Goodenough suggests. That must be left to scholars with full command of the documentary material. An opposing view is expressed by Avi-Yonah (supra n. 2), col. 188, who says of synagogues from the third to eighth century A.D.: "their homogeneity is assured owing to the uniform worship they served, and to a large extent also by their geographical proximity."

66. See Kraeling's discussion of the influence of Mesopotamian domestic and religious architecture on the Dura synagogue in the section "Synagogue Types and Structural Principles," *Final Report* (supra n. 1), 20-25. The view is expressed most directly on pp. 22-23, that in its general form and organization the House of Assembly at Dura "can be explained as a derivative of the domestic architecture of Mesopotamia," but that the aedicula "seems to depend directly upon contemporary religious edifices" (p. 22) ... "The aedicula of the Dura Synagogue is related structurally at least to the religious architecture of the later Orient generally speaking" (p. 23).

67. *Ibid.*, 33. He cites literature on the question of Babylonian vs. Palestinian origins of the synagogue as an institution in n. 155 on that page. Also, he refers to analogies between the Dura building and synagogues of Babylonia in p. 23, n. 106. Goodenough (supra n. 1), IX, 8-10, "Dura and Babylonian Jews," questions the view that Judaism at Dura resembled the Judaism of the Babylonian communities.

68. Kraeling, *Final Report* (supra n. 1), 13; similarly on pp. 32-33.

69. Goodenough (supra n. 1), IX, 29, notes that "on the whole, the colonnade rarely appears in the courtyards of Dura houses, and none is shown on Pearson's plan of a 'typical private house'." His conclusion (IX, 29-30; also IX, 15, X, 198) is that the courtyard and the aedicula of the Dura synagogue were both derived from forms established in the pagan temples of the city. He cites examples of local temples (plans in vol. XI, figs. 3-5, 7) which he says show "the colonnades used in a way very much like the Jewish sanctuary in Dura," but in none of the examples cited do the columns form a peristyle court; the parallel is far-fetched.

70. Kraeling, *Final Report* (supra n. 1), 334.

71. *Ibid.*, p. 21, n. 91.

The three Dura volumes are the final—one may even say the crowning—section of the whole. As Goodenough's work was based on a definite thesis we should approach it on two planes: we must first ask ourselves what the author intended to prove, and then how he set about doing it. In this case we might profitably reverse the usual order: first take his thesis for granted and inquire into the method, and at a later stage examine the validity of the thesis itself. It is only fair to add that, as we are sitting, so to speak, in judgment on a venerated teacher's way of handling the evidence, we cannot justly blame him for failing to take into account material discovered after his labors had been concluded and which he could not therefore possibly have taken into consideration.

Let us then first dwell on the positive side of Goodenough's treatment of the Dura paintings. Any examination of even well-known material by a critical, well-trained and scholarly mind is bound to result in some of the factors being seen in a new light. We shall limit ourselves to but a few of Goodenough's penetrating and just observations. For instance he noted the curious parallelism between the embryonic mask of the infant Moses in the Nilotic scene and that of the widow's son revived by the prophet Elijah.[1] On many occasions Goodenough has been able to demonstrate the soundness of his judgment, even if this implied dissent from the majority of his colleagues. He has for instance seen, rightly in our opinion, that the fragmentary panel of the man in a "civilian" dress who is untying his shoes, opposite the "Burning Bush" scene in the four panels near the niche in the west wall,[2] can only refer to Moses on Mount Horeb—for the only possible competitor, Joshua (with reference to Joshua 5:13-15), would almost invariably appear in military garb. The fact of Moses untying his shoes also when receiving the Law on Mount Sinai was a commonplace assumption in Byzantine iconography; it is only by accident that this fact was taken for granted by the biblical account and is not mentioned expressly in the Book of Exodus. Goodenough drew the logical conclusion that all four panels around the niche represented Moses, and Moses only (fig. 1).

Another of his identifications, that of Orpheus with David,[3] has been brilliantly vindicated by the discovery of the Gaza synagogue mosaic pavement (dated 509) in which a royal figure is shown surrounded by animals, while playing the lyre, and is described expressly as "David."[4] Goodenough's interpretation of the last scene in the Ezekiel series as representing the legendary story of the execution of the prophet, seems to us to be both logical and consistent, although there is as yet no textual proof for it.[5]

We may now pass on to the debit side of the

methodological balance sheet. Our misgivings begin as
soon as we examine in detail the way in which Goodenough tried to buttress his main thesis of the symbolical value of the images and ornaments as expressions of an alleged "mystical" Judaism. Like that of
most men led on by a vision, his scholarly judgment
on what is and what is not evidence is sometimes at
fault. Like Faust, who, having swallowed the Meph-
istophelian potion, sees Fair Helen in every woman,
Goodenough tended to see his mystic symbolism everywhere. It is a sad proof of human fallibility that
our revered master reproached others with his own
failings. Thus for instance, Rachel Wischnitzer is
guilty of seeing "Messianism" in all manifestations of
Jewish art.[6] Verily, this is a case of "beholding a
mote in his brother's (or rather sister's) eye but not
the beam in his own" (Matthew 7:3).

To take but one example of methodological failing, let us examine the discussion of the dresses represented in the Dura paintings.[7] Holding firmly to his
fundamental tenet "In the beginning there was the
logos"—of Philo of course—Goodenough chases the
use of the white himation and the chiton ornamented
with *clavi* for page after page through the pagan and
Christian centuries. For here there are the men in
shining white for which there are Philonic parallels.
On the other hand the even more numerous personages in Parthian dress, including King David himself,

get relatively short shrift. To come down to a point of detail: Goodenough noted the importance of the bar-shaped notched signs (*gammas*) which appear on the himatia at Dura and elsewhere.[8] They are indeed significant, but not in the way he assumed. For it has been conclusively proved by Yadin on the basis of his finds in the Judean desert caves that these marks served to distinguish between male and female garments, these being in all other respects identical in shape and texture. As according to Deuteronomy 22:5 women were not allowed to wear male garments, the two had to be distinguished in some way by the pious. The male signs are straight bars, the female the angled ones.[9]

I cite one more example for the drawing of convenient conclusions on the basis of selected evidence, disregarding inconvenient facts. In describing the left side of the panel over the niche in the western wall, Goodenough noted the absence of two of the symbols which usually accompany the seven branched lampstand (*menorah*) in synagogal art, that is the *shofar* and the incense shovel. The latter he disregarded, but the alleged omission of the *shofar* leads him to far-reaching conclusions—in particular that the "Offering of Isaac" as represented on the right side of the same panel represents the "mystic" equivalent of the *shofar*.[10] Not having ever had the privilege of examining the original, we cannot be certain of the

following observation. It seems however from a study
of the photographs published that there are faint
traces of a *shofar* and perhaps even of the incense
shovel in the apparently empty space to the left of
the *menorah*.[11] If this is a fact, the whole elaborate
parallelism with the "Offering of Isaac" falls to the
ground (fig. 1).

Another example of how one can be misled by
the mystic will o' the wisp is the following. In discussing the appearance of the philosopher (or rather the
philosopher's garb) on later Roman sarcophagi, Goodenough describes one such example.[12] He explains
that the man "seems to be giving the saving instruc-
tions or mystic knowledge or *gnosis* to the veiled lady
beside him." Unfortunately for this thesis the lady
happens to be Demeter, who appears on this
sarcophagus together with Artemis and the Dioscuri.
Clearly the sage in the center would be much more in
need of mystic instruction from the great goddess of
the Eleusiac mysteries than the other way round.

In the paintings in the Dura Mithraeum[13] two
figures are represented in Persian dress, each holding a
scroll. This is in fact the most common way of indicat-
ing a personage of importance in the Greco-Roman
world. Goodenough however assumes—without proof
—that these scrolls were "containing, one must suppose, the mystic secrets."

In the same way the common rosette becomes a

symbol of the "sun and stars";[14] in the dado of Dura
the female masks predominate and the male ones are
subordinated[15]—a conclusion based on less than half
of the material, the other half of the dado having
been destroyed. Yet this evidence is supposed to suf-
fice for a far-reaching theory.

In this way conclusions are arrived at not *ex
fortiori* but *ex infirmoire*—one weak link serving to
support a still weaker one and so forth. For example,
we all know from the Bible (Esther 6:8-11) that
Mordecai was arrayed by Ahasuerus' orders in a royal
apparel—and so he appears in the Dura painting. This
makes him—according to Goodenough—a "mystic"
king; and a mystic king is a god; and so the riding
Mordecai become a projection of the cavalier god.[16]
In the same picture Esther is dressed like a Tyche,
and Tyche equals Atargatis; hence Esther is a projection of Atargatis[17] (fig. 6).

As we all know, God is never represented in
Jewish and early Christian figurative art (if we except
some of the sarcophagi) as a human being. The divine
power is only hinted at by the representation of a
hand emerging from heaven. The Dura artists, for all
their or their patrons' "liberal" attitude have followed this convention in the Exodus pictures, in the
Elijah and Ezekiel cycles, etc. How are we to understand the suggestion made by Goodenough,[18] even if
timidly made, that the "Throne" to which the mystic

vine is leading in the reredos is a Throne occupied by
a mystic Triad? Does the figure in Parthian garb on
the Throne represent God Himself?

Thus far we have only dealt with the methodological side of Goodenough's work, noting the
strength and weakness of his approach to his subject.
We should now consider his basic tenet—the theory
of a "mystical" Judaism. Goodenough has assumed
that the literary expressions of this Jewish mysticism
—always apart from the invaluable Philo—had been in
later centuries victims of rabbinical censorship, and
were thus lost, especially as the Christian church was
not interested in their preservation as happened to
the Books of the Maccabees or the works of Josephus
Flavius. In his eyes, however, the proof of the
existence of this mystical Judaism was preserved in
the visible symbols of Jewish art in the Talmudic
period.

We are approaching now the core of Goodenough's work and it behoves us to tread warily, step
by step.

Firstly, it is undeniable that there existed a
Jewish religious symbolism and imagery in antiquity,
and that much of it was derived from the symbols
and images current in the Greco-Roman environment.
When the Jewish leaders abandoned the strict interpretation of the Second Commandment which was
dominant in the period of the Second Temple and

after, they allowed a freer use of human and animal forms (at least in two dimensional representations). More borrowing of forms can be noticed then from the Gentile imagery. The points in dispute are the values underlying such symbols: were they purely Jewish in the orthodox sense, or did they keep their non-Jewish meaning, or did they express some intermediate value common to both Gentiles and Jews?

To make our meaning clear, let us take a modern parallel. Let us imagine a war memorial, topped by a cross, with the figure of a mourning victory—represented in the usual shape of a winged woman— crouching below. Let us further assume that the memorial is found after two thousand years by some archaeologists of the future. How are they to tell that the cross represented in its time a living faith, whereas the victory was a type borrowed from a religion dead a long time before the erection of the monument? In the same way, the problem of what was a living religious symbol and what a purely decorative element cannot be solved by assuming that every single decorative or figurative detail was the expression of a deep religious meaning, whether direct or transposed. The classical proof of this fact is the synagogue pavement of Ma'on (Nirim) found in the vicinity of Gaza and dated to the middle sixth century.[19] The southern part of the synagogue, that further removed from Jerusalem, shows a pattern of vine trellis growing out

of an amphora, flanked by peacocks, and with various
animals and offering vases within the medallions
formed by the trellis. Had the synagogue authorities
of that time been well versed in their "Goodenough,"
they would have understood the symbolic value of
these elements (fig. 9), which are repeated *ad
nauseaṁ* in Byzantine church pavements. The
amphora and vine are evidence of the "divine
fluid,"[20] the peacocks symbols of immortality,[21]
and so on. However these benighted ignoramuses did
not think so; they ordered from the mosaic workshop
of Gaza which made this pavement (and which
worked for churches and synagogues with the same
pattern books; witness the pavements at Ma'on and
Shellal)[22] to prepare a special wedge, full of what
they must have regarded as specific *Jewish* symbols
and which they must have ordered specially. These
include the seven-branched lampstand, the lions, the
palm trees, *ethrog*, *shofar*, etc. All these were inserted
in the northern, holier, end of the pavement, that
nearest to the Shrine of the Torah Scrolls and that
pointing to Jerusalem. This example should serve as a
warning against assuming that transitory symbolical
values, good for their own period and environment,
can be transferred to another without losing their
meaning. Symbols stand for certain values, and
certain times, and are not good for all eternity.

Hence the victories supporting a garland in the

Rama or Kafr Bir'am synagogues,[23] and even those on the temple painted at Dura,[24] do not mean the same as the victories (identical in form but quite different in meaning) on the triumphal arches of Titus or Septimius Severus. The latter stand for the triumph of the emperor, the former for that of the faith of his victims. The staff of Moses in the Exodus scenes at Dura[25] looks like the club of Hercules; but this can hardly mean that Moses is Hercules in disguise. It is an indication in visual language that he wrought great deeds like the pagan strongman. Just as the translators of the Septuagint used the Greek koiné to express the Hebrew scriptural faith, so did the artists and their Jewish patrons use the common artistic convention of the period to say their orthodox say and no other.

As regards the "inspirational" background of the Dura paintings, that is to say the choice of the place of origin of Jewish figurative art (among Alexandria, Antioch and Babylonia), Goodenough was, in our opinion, on the right track. For all the formal Parthian influences visible in them, the Dura paintings could hardly be conceived in the local Babylonian atmosphere, notwithstanding the reference here and there to works of art among the Jews of Babylonia. The basic material of the paintings is Hellenistic, not Oriental in its character and the choice lies between Antioch and Alexandria. Goodenough chose the

latter, as the center of Jewish Philonic mysticism
which in his opinion inspired the paintings. We
believe him to be right, if for the wrong reason. If we
try to trace the various aspects of early Jewish visual
art, as reflected in the catacomb paintings, the
mosaics in churches and synagogues, the Bible manuscripts, the sarcophagus reliefs, the ivory reliefs, etc.,
they appear, for all their local variations, to have
originated in one place and time. They seem to have
been part of the tremendóus effort made by the
Hellenized Jews — mainly Alexandrian — to make
Judaism respectable, or even attractive, in the eyes of
the Gentiles by giving it a Greek form. The Bible in
its Hebrew form, or even in the Septuagint transla-
tion, was too sacred to be illustrated figuratively.
However the biblical stories could be transformed
into epic poems, tragedies and other forms of Greek
literary expression. There could be no reasonable
objection against the illumination of these stories in
the Hellenistic manner, which had just begun to
spread in the Greek world under Egyptian influence.
The cycle of images thus elaborated was based mainly
on Greek mythological representations (Adam and
Eve and the Serpent as Jason and Medea with the
dragon, Noah as Danae, Jonah as Endymion, etc.). It
was thus formally Hellenistic and the main biblical
heroes have kept their Hellenistic dress, the chiton,
himation and sandals, throughout the times deep into

the Middle Ages, as can still be seen in the mosaics of
San Marco and Monreale. The minor figures were,
however, from early times, adapted to the local circumstances. This explains *inter alia* the differences in
costume observable at Dura. The formal origin of this
type of representation was Alexandrine; the style of
the paintings with their hierarchic perspective,
isocephaly, frontality, etc., belong to the third
century, the style of the period when the murals were
painted, and to their semi-Oriental milieu. They stand
at the point of transition between classical and late
classical art. Goodenough's theological and philosophical training caused his lack of interest in the
history of art and in the formal aspect of the Dura
paintings—this point does in fact require still much
further study.

It seems that Goodenough evolved his theory of a
"mystic" Judaism in order to reconcile the undeniable fact that the Jews of Dura (and elsewhere in that
period, if we except the Judaeo-Christians) were
"good Jews" in the mainstream of Judaism in the
orthodox sense, and that they yet used at the same
time a symbolic imagery which meant again something else to non-Jews. No scholar, however conscien-
tious, can entirely escape conditioning by his environment and his period. For Goodenough this meant the
belief in one basic religious essence (a belief common
in America and now spreading elsewhere under the

influence of American theology). This essential substance is, in that view, shared by all the faiths of the
world, however diverse in their superstructures. To
one not familiar with this concept, Goodenough
seems again and again to try to infiltrate Christian
elements, such as the Trinity, the sacred bread and
wine etc., into Judaism by way of his interpretation of the "mystic" symbolism. For instance in the
original form of the reredos painting above the Torah
niche in the Dura synagogue there was a table with a
"round object" and another with an amphora—
symbols, according to Goodenough—of the "divine
loaf of bread" and the "divine fluid." Again the figures above in the later stages of this painting are
interpreted as the "Great Three" and the Jewish deity
at the same time.[26] On another occasion he states
plainly that if a symbol has a certain meaning in
Christianity "there is a good reason to suppose that it
meant the same in Judaism."[27] These and similar
utterances are not, however, an attempt to smuggle
eucharistic values into the ritual of the synagogue,
but *bona fide* expressions of a belief in a common
mystic faith uniting all mankind. In any case even at
Dura the "round object" and the amphora were later
on painted over and replaced by images of Jacob
blessing his sons and grandsons. After all as the
fathers of this alleged "symbolism" lived in the third
century and not in the nineteenth or twentieth, they

were probably unaware of the parallels suggested.

Two recent discoveries have considerably shaken Goodenough's theory of a "mystic" as opposed to a normative Judaism. One was that of the necropolis at Beth She'arim in Western Galilee. This place was selected as the burial place of the sainted patriarch Judah I (died ca. 217). After that many Jews from Palestine and even from the eastern Diaspora, from Palmyra to Himyar in Arabia, were desirous of being buried near the patriarch's monumental sepulchre (probably catacomb No. 14 at Beth She'arim).[28] Especially significant for our subject is Catacomb No. 20, which is not far from No. 14 and which like the latter has a special praying space above its entrance. Catacomb No. 20 is a burial cave of huge dimensions containing over 300 burials. Most of these are in decorated stone coffins locally made; a minority was probably buried in reused pagan sarcophagi with mythological scenes. To judge from the inscriptions, among those buried in this cave were members of the patriarchal family, famous rabbis (some even called "Holy"). Yet the coffins in this cave appear again and again decorated with a plethora of "mystic" symbols. Almost the whole repertoire of Goodenough's first eight volumes can be found here—Jewish symbols, pagan symbols, etc. Typical in this respect is coffin No. 117 of Gamaliel the son of Rabbi Eleazar with its rich figurative "symbolical" ornament.[29] These burials are of people apparently closely connected with the patriarchal house, the leaders of the Sanhedrin and of "normative" Judaism—and yet they use "mystic" symbols in decorating their burials.

The same attitude can be observed in the second discovery we would like to mention in this context— that of the synagogue at Hammath-Tiberias (the second in this locality), which is dated to the first half of the fourth century.[30] The mosaic pavement of this synagogue includes images of the signs of the Zodiac, which were taken over directly from Greek prototypes. Virgo is Kore with her torch, Libra is Minos with his scepter, Apollo-Helios appears in the center of the Zodiac complete with his chariot. Yet among the dedicants is one who describes himself as the *"trephos* of the most illustrious patriarchs," at that time residing at Tiberias, only a mile away. The whole resembles nothing as much as an (imaginary) discovery of a Protestant church and cemetery within the confines of Vatican City. Were the patriarchs, the heads of rabbinical Jewry, unorthodox "mystics?"

We can only conclude that the alleged antagonism between "mystic" and "normative" Judaism is a later purely theoretical construction. The relative absence of a literature of mysticism in early Jewish sources or of a full treatment of the problems of mysticism in the pages of the Talmud are a mere *argumentum ex silentio*, with little probative value—

one might as soon look for traces of French Romanticism in the Code Napoleon. We believe that much more mystic material can be found in talmudic and midrashic literature than is quoted by Goodenough who was unfortunately unable to consult the original texts. In short we cannot isolate in the manner of a chemist or biologist the "mystic" and "normative" elements of Judaism in a *Reinkultur*. All religion involves a mystic element and there were Jewish mystics among the rabbis of the Talmudic period. Goodenough has rightly pointed out the existence of this mystic trend in Judaism in the Greco-Roman period in its visual form; but we need not separate this trend from the many others which went to make up the rich religious life of the Talmudic period—one of the great creative eras of Judaism. His great achievement was to draw our attention away from the texts, on which Jewish scholarship had been almost exclusively focused, to the world of images, and thus to restore to Judaism a visual dimension it had sadly lacked before.

1. E. R. Goodenough: *Jewish Symbols in the Greco-Roman Period* IX-XI: *Symbolism in the Dura Synagogue* (New York, 1964) [henceforward by volume and page alone], IX, 200, and 228.

2. XI, pl. V.

3. IX, 93ff.

4. A. Ovadiah, *Israel Exploration Journal* 19 (1969), 193, pl. 15.

5. X, 185ff.

6. IX, 227 n. 5.

7. IX, 124ff.

8. IX, 88.

9. Y. Yadin, *Bar Kokhba* (London, 1971), 69ff. Actually only the marks on the women's garments can be properly called *gammas.*

10. IX, 75f.

11. XI, fig. 66.

12. IX, 146 and XI, fig. 137.

13. XI, fig. 140 and IX, 147.

15. IX, 61.

16. IX, 180.

17. IX, 179.

18. IX, 88.

19. M. Avi-Yonah, *Bulletin of the Louis M. Rabinowitz Fund*
     3 (1960), 25ff.

20. IX, 145, 205.

21. IX, 57.

22. *Op. cit.*, n. 19 above, 32ff.

23. Goodenough III, figs. 510, 555; cf. figs. 524, 525.

24. XI, pls. X, XI.

25. XI, pl. XIV.

26. IX, 82, 88.

27. IX, 53.

28. N. Avigad, *Israel Exploration Journal* 5 (1955), 218ff.

29. Id., *ib.*, 7 (1957), 89 and Beth Shearim III (Jerusalem,
     1971), 79.

30. M. Dothan in *Encyclopaedia of Excavations in the Holy
     Land*, s.v. (Hebrew).

PROGRAMMATIC PAINTING IN THE DURA SYNAGOGUE

Joseph Gutmann

Many attempts have been made in the last forty years to discover the meaning and purpose of the Dura-Europos paintings. Basically, scholars have taken one of three positions:

a. that there is no unifying idea behind the cycle of paintings;

b. that there is one governing theological theme underlying the paintings;

c. that there are several diverse messages expressed.

A. Rostovtzeff, Sukenik and Leveen see no governing idea behind the cycle of paintings. They feel that the individual panels merely related to special liturgical readings of the Sabbath and the festivals and enabled the worshippers to visualize some of the episodes as they were being read and interpreted in the synagogue.

B. Scholars, such as Grabar, Sonne, Wischnitzer and Goodenough, find a unified theological theme reflected in the cycle of paintings. Grabar finds that the scenes are a tribute to the Sovereignty of God—analogous to programs found in Roman Imperial art.

With respect to the second figural band, which will be
our major concern, Grabar concludes that his idea is
manifest here through the power of the ark, God's
sacred palladium, which brings to naught the plans of
hostile rulers. Sonne believes the saying of Rabbi
Simon reflected in the Dura paintings: "There are
three crowns: The crown of Torah, the crown of
Priesthood and the crown of Kingdom" (*Avoth* 4.17).
Hence, for him, the second band spells out the crown
of Priesthood with Aaron as the dominant figure.
Wischnitzer sees the messianic drama pervading the
whole body of paintings. The second band, according
to her interpretation, has the story of the ark, symbolic of the trials and tribulations that will usher in
the messianic era. Goodenough claims that the
Philonic doctrine of the soul's mystic ascent to true
being and the hope of victory over death is reflected
not only in the second band, but in all the paintings.

C.   Du Mesnil du Buisson and Kraeling, rather
than seeing a unified idea, see the cycle containing
many diverse religious themes. Du Mesnil du Buisson,
classifying the paintings by subject matter, feels that
the second band is liturgical—dealing with the covenant
relationship between God and Israel, which expresses
itself in cultic performance. Kraeling suggests that the
paintings reveal such themes as the historical covenant relationship, reward and punishment, salvation
and messianic expectation.[1]

Although differing widely in their interpretation of the cycle of paintings, scholars, with the exception of Goodenough, are generally agreed that any explanation of the paintings must be rooted in contemporary rabbinic Judaism. They differ as to whether that rabbinic Judaism might have been a "normative legalistic Judaism" or an "eschatological-material mysticism." Goodenough and his disciples maintain that the paintings can only be understood in terms of a mystic Hellenistic Judaism.

"The question is," said Alice in Lewis Carroll's *Through the Looking-Glass*, "whether you can make words mean so many different things." The same sentiments can easily be applied to the Dura paintings. Each scholar finds a different meaning in the cycle depending on the conceptual framework he brings to his interpretation, so that in reading these widely divergent reconstructions we are not always certain that the same synagogue is being discussed.

Kraeling has rightly rejected many of the above proffered interpretations, which would impose a scholarly straitjacket on the cycle of paintings. Kraeling's own conclusions, however, as Moses Hadas pointed out, leave the reader with "a sense of bafflement . . . surely something more is involved than a discontinuous series of crude representations of Bible stories . . . there are layers of meaning perceptible only by a different key."[2] Before suggesting a new approach to this complex and difficult problem, let us briefly summarize what scholars generally agree on with respect to the iconography of the cycle and the specific scenes of the second band.

Scholars agree:

1. That Dura was not an intellectual center, but an undistinguished frontier town whose Roman garrison was posted there to stave off a Sasanian attack. The small Jewish community of Dura lived primarily as merchants providing supplies to the Roman army.

2. That the repertoire of the Dura synagogue may have been repeated with greater artistic skill in no-longer extant or buried synagogues in some major Near Eastern Jewish centers.

3. That the paintings do not follow the narrative sequence of the Bible, but present an apparently disordered array of biblical scenes drawn from various books of the Bible.

4. That many of the scenes contain non-biblical homiletical embellishments, called *aggadoth*.

The identification of the individual panels of the second band, beginning with the panel to the left of the Torah shrine on the west side, can be summarized, as follows:

1. General agreement that this is a composite scene dealing with the Consecration of the Tabernacle and its priests. Disagreement is restricted to two other identifications—Aaron   and   his   sons   consecrated

(Wischnitzer); open mystic Temple of the priests (Goodenough).[3]

2. Some scholars feel that this is a composite scene of the Well in the Wilderness. Based on a well-known legend, found also in Christian literature and Byzantine art and known to Muhammad (*Sura* 7.100), the panel shows a rock-well which followed the Israelites in the wilderness and set itself up before the Tabernacle at each new encampment. A stream or spring flowed from the single rock to each of the twelve tribes.[4] Disagreement among scholars is as follows: Well of Be'er (Kraeling), Wells of Elim (Sonne), Moses giving the law (Wischnitzer), Feast of Tabernacles (du Mesnil du Buisson)[5] (fig. 2).

3. *South Side.* I would suggest Crossing of the Jordan with the ark under Joshua—a scene that plays a prominent role in later church art, such as in the 5th century cycle of S. Maria Maggiore, Rome; the Joshua Rotulus of the 10th century, and the 11th-12th century Octateuchs, all harking back to lost, earlier models.[6]

Other suggestions by scholars are: Aaron's death (Sonne), Joseph's bones carried to Canaan (Wischnitzer), Dedication of Solomon's Temple (Kraeling)[7] (fig. 3).

4. *North Side.* General agreement that the Sanctuary of Shiloh is represented. Disagreement only as to whether Hannah and the child Samuel or Eli and

Samuel are depicted (I Samuel 1 or 3).[8]

5. General agreement that the Battle of Eben-Ezer and the capture of the ark by the Philistines (I Samuel 4) is shown[9] (fig. 4).

6. *West Side.* General agreement that the ark in the land of the Philistines is portrayed (I Samuel 5-6).[10]

7. Most scholars agree that the Temple of Solomon at Jerusalem is shown. Disagreement ranges from identifying the panel as Beth-Shemesh (Wischnitzer), the Restored Temple of Josiah (Grabar, Leveen), the Closed Mystic Temple (Goodenough),[11] to the Heavenly Temple[12] (fig. 5).

8. The two figures flanking the Sanctuaries probably represent biblical figures—it is difficult to determine which. Suggestions for the figure with the scroll are: Ezra (Kraeling), Samuel or Nathan (Wischnitzer), Jeremiah (du Mesnil du Buisson), Moses (Goodenough). The figure with hands crossed has been identified as: Abraham (Kraeling), Joshua (Sukenik), Enoch (Kümmel), Jacob (Sonne), Moses (Goodenough) (fig. 1).

The artist shows us, on the right, a figure in classical stance reading or exposing the sacred law. The huge scroll forms a cross with the body, largely subordinating the body to it, and emphasizing thereby the importance of the sacred book—the Torah.[13] The other figure, on the left, as Kraeling has already

observed, wears the himation in an unusual way. It is
draped over the shoulders and covers both arms and is
gathered together in front of the body in such a way
that the folded ends hang down from the crossed and
covered hands.[14] This crossing of the covered hands
and the rigid stance convey an impression of
humility, adoration or supplication. Indeed, the
covered hands are familiar from later Christian art
and in a contemporary source we read that Raba
"removed his cloak, folded his hands and prayed, saying '(I pray) like a slave before his master' " (*Babylonian Talmud*, *Shabbath* 10a).

Hence, the two personages may be biblical
figures in the acts of prayer and reading of Scripture.

Returning to the second band, we can make
several general observations:

1. That this band is the largest of the three figurative bands—measuring 4'9" (1.53 m.), as against 4'3"
(1.30 m.) for the first band and 3'10" (1.16 m.) for
the upper band.

2. That the hand of God is not found intervening
in any of the preserved panels of the second band,
although it is prominently featured in other paintings.
Here, God's presence seems to be indicated by the
implied or actual presence of the ark.

3. That it deals with the history of the ark—its
power and its vicissitudes—beginning with its role in
the cult of the Wilderness Tabernacle and culminating

with its enshrinement in the Temple of Solomon. We see it crossing the Jordan under Joshua, as well as being captured by the Philistines. We note the miracles it performed directly at the Temple of Dagon in Philistia and indirectly through the miraculous well in the wilderness.

4. That the flat biblical ark-box (as in the Joshua mosaic scenes in S. Maria Maggiore, Rome) is always depicted in Dura as a tall yellow Torah ark-chest with rounded top, although the artist felt free to vary the details of the decorations from scene to scene.[15]

Given all of these facts, what possible key for unlocking the program can be offered? Let us state at the outset that we will not, or better, cannot hypothecate the precise kind of Judaism that flourished at Dura. No other similar synagogue has been found, no contemporary texts are available to explain the program, and the primary literary documents on hand are of such a nature that they yield few clues to help us understand the many regional variations of the dominent, prevailing Judaism of that period. What is still greatly misunderstood and should be pointed out is the fact that Dura belongs to a radically new type of Judaism that had emerged much earlier, out of which Christianity grew and was nourished. This new Judaism had substituted prayers within synagogues for sacrifices at the Temple. It elevated the scholar-rabbi and did away with priestly

intermediaries. It offered eternal life through personal
salvation of the soul and bodily resurrection, rather
than promising fertility of the land. It developed a
new system of authority based on a revealed two-fold
Law—the Written and the Oral—in preference to the
Pentateuch, the authoritative text of the priest-
ly-Temple centered Judaism.

Within the new Oral Law, we find no connected
historical narrative or biography, as is the case in the
Bible. In fact, the "Old Testament" or biblical text
was no longer viewed as a literal document, but as a
divine source for solving contemporary problems. In
the Oral Law, Scriptural proof was now adduced to
illumine a non-biblical concept, be it in the form of a
moral teaching or a law. Combining verses and stories,
drawn from different biblical books, preferring an
aggadic elaboration over a biblical fact, was now
simply a means to make the point of an identical
lesson and to prove the essential unity and timeless-
ness of God's entire revelation.[16]

If Dura belongs within the orbit of this new type
of Judaism, are the "Old Testament" stories here too
used simply as prooftexts with the purpose of driving
home a non-biblical context—a new theological concept, liturgy or teaching? Already in late pagan art,
we find that Greek mythological stories are used
without regard to their original narrative sequence. As
in Dura, they probably served as prooftexts to spell

out and underwrite in an analogous fashion a new liturgical-theological context or program of the contemporary mystery religions.[17]

In later Christianity, as for instance in the 5th century church of S. Maria Maggiore in Rome [18] and the 6th century church of San Vitale in Ravenna[19] there is no doubt that the Old Testament scenes, torn out of the sequential narrative confines of the Bible, are analogously used to underwrite the new liturgical-theological program of contemporary Christianity.

A religious building, such as Dura, it must be stressed, should be analyzed on two levels:

a. the architectural and artistic significance of the visible, physical structure;

b. the now lost, invisible, active liturgical function —the rites, ceremonial movements and prayers—which the building and its art were created to shelter.

In such churches as S. Vitale, Ravenna, we know that the main function of the building and its art was to give meaning to the "liturgy of the Eucharist." This is manifest in the mosaic in the apse of the presbytery which shows the procession of the clergy, led by the bishop, and followed by the emperor and empress and their entourage, as they enter into the nave of the church.[20] On the choir walls we find mosaics of Abel and Melchizedek sharing a church altar between them on which are bread and wine. On the other side, we see three angels seated before another church altar with bread marked by crosses and a wine kantharos. The angels are visiting Abraham, who offers them the calf. Sarah is in the doorway of the tent; Abraham to the right is about to sacrifice Isaac. Both mosaics flank and are above the real church altar below where the Eucharist was celebrated by the officiating priest.[21] All the Old Testament biblical figures are placed on the walls as antitypes, or proofs, of Christ's Passion, and are united by the Canon of the Mass—the prayer text of offering after the wine and bread are consecrated. Hence, all these biblical figures in the lunettes, torn out of their historical biblical context, are related nevertheless, but to a new context—the words of the mass celebrated at the altar below:

> Be pleased to look upon these offerings with a gracious and favorable countenance, accept them even as You were pleased to accept the offerings of Your just servant Abel, the sacrifice of Abraham, our patriarch, and that of Melchizedek, Your high priest—a holy sacrifice, a spotless victim.[21a]

Does the substitution at Dura of the Torah ark-chest, which houses the most important object of the synagogue—the Torah, symbolic of God's entire revelation—serve a purpose similar to that of the S. Vitale altar-table, where the most important rite of the Church is performed? Do the biblical scenes and

flanking figures in the second band, torn out of their
biblical context, serve as proofs of a new theological
context and are they similarly bound together by the
words of an actual liturgical celebration? I believe so.

We have fragments of a hymn, recorded by Isaac
Nappaha, a mid-third-century Palestinian scholar
(*amora*), which, according to Louis Ginzberg, was un-
questionably sung by the congregation during the
entrance procession of the Torah ark.[22] In the early
synagogue, the Torah-ark was kept in a room outside
the synagogue and was only brought in for synagogal
worship.[23] The hymn, placed in the text, in the
mouths of the kine bringing back the captured ark
from Philistia, reads:

> Sing, O sing, acacia (shrine)
> Ascend in the fullness of your majesty
> Bedecked with golden embroidery
> Praised in the sanctuary-palace
> Adorned with the finest ornaments
> *(Babylonian Talmud, Avodah Zarah 24b).*

The acacia-shrine poetically refers to the ark;
devir-armon (sanctuary-palace) may be an allusion to
the Torah niche, the synagogue nave or room.[24] It
has already been noted that the Dura scene of the ark
in the land of the Philistines is related to this hymn;
that the ark is regally enthroned on cushions—"in the
fullness of your majesty"—and shows analogies to
Sasanian royal cosmic thrones on wheels.[25] To my

knowledge, however, only Ginzberg perceived that this text was part of an actual liturgical hymn, although he was unaware of its link to Dura.[26]

If our interpretation is correct, the congregation recounted through song in the actual liturgical ark procession what is depicted on the second band of the wall—the history, vicissitudes and miracles of the ark. In contemporary literature there is an implied association between the synagogal Torah ark and the Tabernacle/Temple ark. The miracles of the ark that we see on the wall occurred, according to the rabbis, because the *Shekhinah* (God's Presence) and *Torah* (God's Revelation) were in the ark.[27] What unites these apparently disorganized scenes then, and what explains the prominence of the synagogal Torah ark in these depictions are not the literal biblical stories, but the text of an actual rabbinic liturgical hymn sung during worship. In the procession around the synagogue, the final resting place of the Torah ark was of course not the Temple of Solomon, but the synagogal Torah niche, the true repository of the synagogal ark. The biblical scenes serve here as pious anchors to secure the continued function of the ark and its salvationary power within a new context.

The prophetic or patriarchal biblical figures above the Torah shrine and flanking the Tabernacle/Temple—one at prayer and the other reading of revealing Scripture—are present as biblical proofs of

1. Cf. C. H. Kraeling, *The Synagogue* (New Haven, 1956), 346ff. For additional bibliography, cf. J. Gutmann, "Die Synagoge von Dura-Europos," *Reallexikon zur byzantinischen Kunst* I (1966), 1238-40 and J. Gutmann, ed., *No Graven Images: Studies in Art and the Hebrew Bible* (New York, 1971), XXXVII-XXXIX.

2. M. Hadas, "Pagan and Jew in the Ancient World," *Commentary* 24 (July, 1957), 81.

3. Kraeling, *op. cit.*, 125ff. Cf. also I. Renov, "A View of Herod's Temple from Nicanor's Gate in a Mural Panel of the Dura-Europos Synagogue," *Israel Exploration Journal* 20 (1970), 67-74 and 21 (1971), 220-21.

4. C. O. Nordström, "The Water Miracles of Moses in Jewish Legend and Byzantine Art," *Orientalia Suecana* 7 (1958), 98-109. Cf. D. Mouriki-Charalambous, "The Octateuch Miniatures of the Byzantine Manuscripts of Cosmas Indicopleustes," Unpublished Ph.D. thesis, Princeton University, 1970, 62-70, 225-26, and E. R. Goodenough, *Jewish Symbols in the Greco-Roman Period* X (New York, 1964), 33-34.

5. Kraeling, *op. cit.*, 118ff.

6. J. Kollwitz, "Der Josuazyklus von S. Maria Maggiore," *Römische Quartalschrift* 61 (1966), 105ff.

7. Kraeling, *op. cit.*, 113ff.

8. *Ibid.*, 93ff.

9. *Ibid.*, 95ff.

10. *Ibid.*, 99ff.

11. *Ibid.*, 105ff.

12. J. Goldstein in *Journal of Near Eastern Studies* 28 (1969), 217, for the Heavenly Temple interpretation. Cf. also R. Wischnitzer, "The 'Closed Temple' Panel in the Synagogue of Dura-Europos," *Journal of the American Oriental Society* 91 (1971), 367ff.

13. Kraeling, *op. cit.*, 232ff.

14. *Ibid.*, 235ff.

15. Christian art knows three types of ark representations: a. the flat box-form. b. the round top chest-form. c. the pointed gable shrine-form. Cf. P. Bloch in *Karolingische Kunst*, ed. by W. Braunfels and H. Schnitzler III (Düsseldorf, 1966), 240ff.

16. Cf. E. Rivkin, *The Shaping of Jewish History* (New York, 1971), 42ff.

17. K. Lehmann, "The *Imagines* of the Elder Philostratus," *The Art Bulletin* 23 (1941), 16ff.

18. Cf. S. Spain, "The Program of the Fifth-Century Mosaics of Santa Maria Maggiore," Unpublished Ph.D. thesis, New York University, 1968, 165ff.

19. F. W. Deichmann, *Ravenna, Geschichte und Monumente*

I (Wiesbaden, 1969), 234ff. Cf. Also C. O. Nordström, *Ravennastudien, Ideengeschichtliche ikonographische Untersuchungen über die Mosaiken von Ravenna* (Stockholm, 1953), 102ff.

20. T. F. Mathews, *The Early Churches of Constantinople: Architecture and Liturgy* (University Park and London, 1971), 146ff. Cf. review by A. Grabar in *Cahiers archéologiques* 22 (1972), 242-44.

21. Deichmann, *op. cit.*, 236:
"Die Handlung also beider biblischen Gestalten, die völlig aus ihrem historischen Zusammenhang gelöst sind, bezieht sich hier auf den kirchlichen Altar und damit augenscheinlich auf das Mysterium der Eucharistie."

21.[a] Cf. P. Parsch, *The Liturgy of the Mass* (London, 1961), and A. Fortescue, *The Mass, A Study of the Roman Liturgy* (London and New York, 1950).

22. L. Ginzberg, "Beiträge zur Lexikographie des Jüdisch-Aramaeischen III," *Essays and Studies in Memory of Linda R. Miller*, ed. I. Davidson (New York, 1938), 86-89. Cf. Kraeling, *op. cit.*, 104-05, and G. Scholem, *Jewish Gnosticism, Merkabah Mysticism, and Talmudic Tradition* (New York, 1960), 24ff.

23. E. L. Sukenik, *Ancient Synagogues in Palestine and Greece* (London, 1934), 52; S. Krauss, *Synagogale Altertümer* (Vienna, 1922), 373f., and C. Wendel, *Der Thoraschrein im Altertum* (Halle, 1950).

24. Ginzberg, *op. cit.*, 87; Kraeling, *op. cit.*, 269 mentions

beth arona, a graffito near the Torah niche. Cf. also Krauss, *op. cit.,* 366ff.

25. Goodenough, *op. cit.,* X, 81-82, fig. 262.

26. Ginzberg, *op. cit.,* 87: "Es lässt sich mit Sicherheit behaupten . . . einem Liede angehörten, das beim 'Einzug' der Lade——in alter Zeit wurde dieselbe ausserhalb der Synagoge aufbewahrt, wohin sie nur zum Gottesdienst gebracht wurde——gesungen wurde."

27. *Tanhuma Wa-Yakhel* 7, 131a and *Exodus Rabbah* 50.2.5. Cf. A. M. Goldberg, *Untersuchungen über die Vorstellung von der Schekhinah in der frühen rabbinischen Literatur* (Berlin, 1969), 45, 52, 70, 75, 476, 508.

28. Recitation of prayers *(Shema and Tefillah)* is the same as the offering of sacrifices: Cf. *Berakhot* 15a, 17a, 26b.

29. Torah reading or study is equal to sacrifices: Cf. *Taanith* 27b, *Megillah* 31b, *Menahoth* 110a.

CONTRIBUTORS

CLARK HOPKINS, Professor Emeritus of Classical Art and Archaeology, University of Michigan. Field director of the Dura-Europos excavations and author of *The Early History of Greece, Introduction to Classical Archaeology* and *Topography and Architecture of Seleucia on the Tigris.*

RICHARD BRILLIANT, Professor of Art History and Archaeology, Columbia University. Author of *Gesture and Rank in Roman Art, The Arch of Septimius Severus in the Roman Forum* and *Dura Final Reports: The Paintings* (in preparation).

MARY LEE THOMPSON, Associate Professor of Art History, Manhattanville College. Author of *Programmatic Painting in Pompeii.*

BERNARD GOLDMAN, Professor of Art and Art History, Wayne State University. Author of *The Sacred Portal* and *Reading and Writing in the Arts.*

ANDREW SEAGER, Associate Professor of Architecture, Ball State University. Author of *Final Report on the Sardis Synagogue* (in preparation).

MICHAEL AVI-YONAH, Professor of Archaeology and History of Art, Hebrew University. Author of *Mosaic Pavements in Palestine, Oriental Art in Roman Palestine, The Jews of Palestine in the Talmudic Period, History of Classical Art, A History of the Holy Land.*

JOSEPH GUTMANN, Professor of Art and Art History, Wayne State University. Author of *Jewish Ceremonial Art, Images of the Jewish Past, Beauty in Holiness* and *No Graven Images.*

SELECTED BIBLIOGRAPHY ON THE
DURA SYNAGOGUE

Aubert, M. "Le peintre de la synagogue de Doura," *Gazette des Beaux-Arts* 20 (1938), 1-24.

Du Mesnil du Buisson, R. *Les peintures de la synagogue de Doura-Europos, 245-256 après J.-C.* Rome, 1939.

Ehrenstein, Th. *Über die Fresken der Synagoge von Dura-Europos.* Wien, 1937.

Goodenough, E. R. *Jewish Symbols in the Greco-Roman Period, Symbolism in the Dura Synagogue, Vols. 9-11.* New York, 1964. Reviews by Smith, M. in *Journal of Biblical Literature* 86 (1967), 53-68; Gutmann, J. in *The Reconstructionist* 31 (1965), 20-25; Bickerman, E. in *The Harvard Theological Review* 58 (1965), 127-51 and *Syria* 44 (1967), 131-61.

Grabar, A. "Le thème religieux des fresques de la synagogue de Doura," *Revue de l'histoire des religions* 123 (1941), 143-92 and 124 (1941), 5-35.

Gutmann, J. "Die Synagoge von Dura-Europos," *Reallexikon zur byzantinischen Kunst I* (1966), 1230-40. *No Graven Images, Studies in Art and the Hebrew Bible.* New York, 1971.

Hempel, H. L. "Zum Problem der Anfänge der AT-Illustration," *Zeitschrift für die*

Alttestamentliche Wissenschaft 69 (1957), 103-31.

Hill, E. "Roman Elements in the Settings of the Synagogue Frescoes at Dura," *Marsyas* 1 (1941), 1-15.

Kraeling, C. H. *The Synagogue, Excavations at Dura-Europos, Final Report VIII*, 1. New Haven, 1956.

Kümmel, W. G. "Die älteste religiöse Kunst der Juden," *Judaica* 2 (1946), 1-56.

Leveen, J. "The Wall Paintings at Dura-Europos," in *The Hebrew Bible in Art*. London, 1944.

Nock, A. D. "The Synagogue Murals of Dura-Europos," in *Harry A. Wolfson Jubilee Volume II*. Jerusalem, 1965.

Nordström, C.-O. "The Water Miracles of Moses in Jewish Legend and Byzantine Art," *Orientalia Suecana* 7 (1958), 78-109.

Perkins, A. *The Art of Dura-Europos*. Oxford, 1973.

Riesenfeld, H. "The Resurrection in Ezekiel XXXVII and in the Dura-Europos Paintings," *Uppsala Universitets Arsskrift* 11 (1948), 27-38.

Rosenthal, E. "Some Notes on the Synagogue Paintings in Relation to Late Antique Bookpainting," in *The Illuminations of the Vergilius Romanus*. Zurich, 1972.

Rostovtzeff, M. I. *Dura-Europos and its Art.* Oxford, 1938.

Schneid, O. *The Paintings of the Synagogue at Dura-Europos.* Tel Aviv, 1946 (Hebrew).

Simon, M. "Remarques sur les synagogues à images de Doura et de Palestine," *Recherches d'histoire judéo-chretienne.* Paris, 1962.

Sonne, I. "The Paintings of the Dura Synagogue," *Hebrew Union College Annual* 20 (1947), 255-362.

Stern, H. "The Orpheus in the Synagogue of Dura-Europos," *The Journal of the Warburg and Courtauld Institutes* 21 (1958), 1-6. "Quelques problèmes d'iconographie paléochrétienne et juive," *Cahiers archéologiques* 12 (1962), 99-113.

Sukenik, E. L. *The Synagogue of Dura-Europos and its Paintings.* Jerusalem, 1947 (Hebrew).

Weitzmann, K. "The Illustration of the Septuagint," and "The Question of Jewish Pictorial Sources on Old Testament Illustration," in *Studies in Classical and Byzantine Manuscript Illumination,* ed. by H. L. Kessler, Chicago and London, 1971.

Widengren, G. "Quelques rapports entre Juifs et Iraniens à l'époque des Parthes," *Suppl. to Vetus Testamentum* 4 (1957), 197-241.

Wischnitzer, R. *The Messianic Theme in the Paintings of the Dura Synagogue.* Chicago, 1948.

INDEX

THE DURA-EUROPOS SYNAGOGUE

ILLUSTRATIONS

Dura Synagogue: Central area with Torah shrine, west wall.
(Figure 1)

Dura Synagogue: West wall, south half. (Figure 2)

Dura Synagogue: South wall. (Figure 3)

Dura Synagogue: North wall. (Figure 4)

Dura Synagogue: West wall, north half. (Figure 5)

180

Dura Synagogue painting, west wall: Mordecai and Esther.
(Figure 6)

Dura Synagogue painting, north wall: Parthian costume, Ezekiel. (Figure 7)

182

Dura Synagogue painting, west wall: Parthian costume of High
Priest, Aaron. (Figure 8)

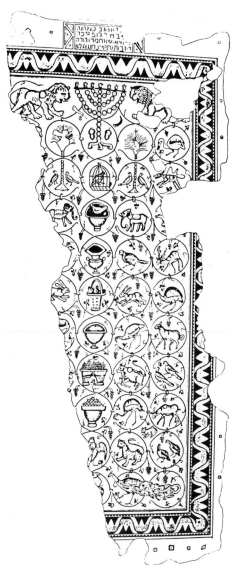

Ma'on (Nirim) Synagogue: Mosaic floor pavement. (Figure 9)

184

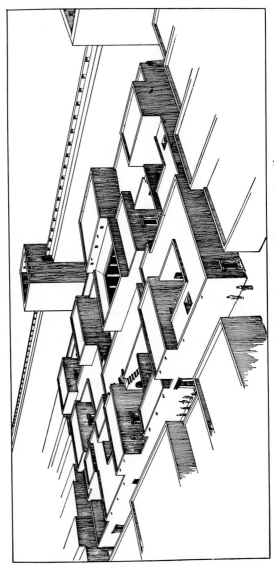

Dura Synagogue: Block L7, isometric reconstruction.
(Figure 10)

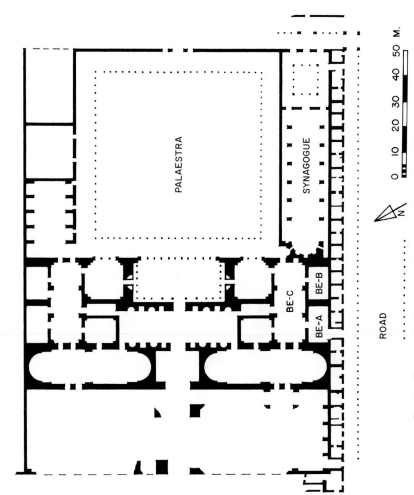

Sardis: Roman bath-gymnasium complex, plan. (Figure 11)

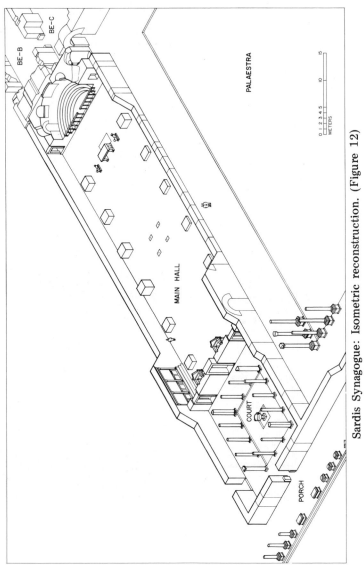

Sardis Synagogue: Isometric reconstruction. (Figure 12)

Sardis Synagogue under restoration, 1971. (Figure 13)

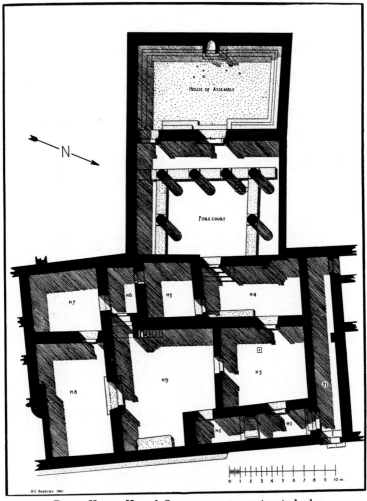

Dura: House H and Synagogue, reconstructed plan.
(Figure 14)

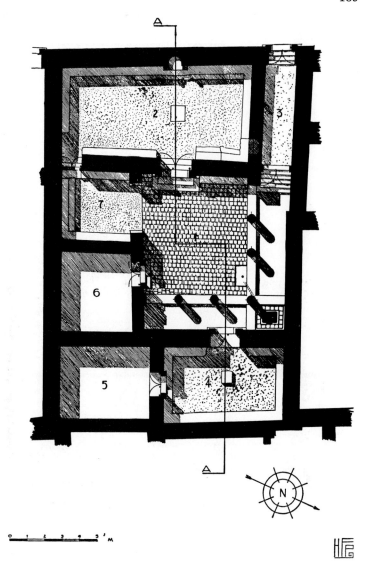

Dura: Earlier Synagogue, reconstructed plan. (Figure 15)

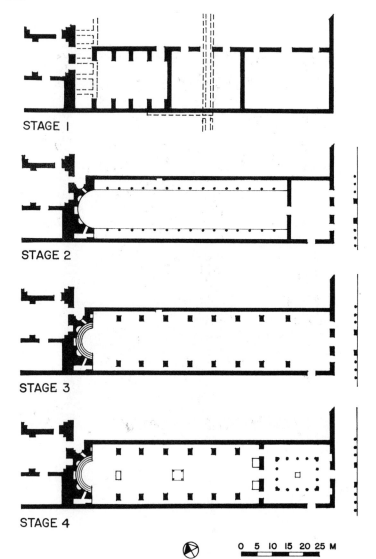

STAGE 1

STAGE 2

STAGE 3

STAGE 4

0 5 10 15 20 25 M

Sardis Synagogue: Stages 1-4, conjectural plans. (Figure 16)